MW00577368

Christianity in the Roman Empire

ROBERT E. WINN

Christianity
in the Roman Empire

Key Figures, Beliefs, and Practices
of the Early Church

AD — 100 — to — 300

HENDRICKSON PUBLISHERS

Christianity in the Roman Empire: Key Figures, Beliefs, and Practices of the
Early Church (AD 100–300)

© 2018 by Robert E. Winn
Hendrickson Publishers Marketing, LLC
P. O. Box 3473
Peabody, Massachusetts 01961-3473
www.hendrickson.com

ISBN 978-1-68307-182-2

Printed in the United States of America

First Printing—November 2018

Cover design by Karol Bailey.
Classical column on cover derived from illustration by iStock.com/lublubachka.

Library of Congress Cataloging-in-Publication

Names: Winn, Robert E., author.
Title: Christianity in the Roman Empire : key figures, beliefs, and practices
    of the early Church (ad 100-300) / Robert E. Winn.
Description: Peabody, MA : Hendrickson Publishers, 2018. | Includes
    bibliographical references.
Identifiers: LCCN 2018028345 | ISBN 9781683071822 (alk. paper)
Subjects: LCSH: Church history--Primitive and early church, ca. 30-600.
Classification: LCC BR165 .W66 2018 | DDC 270.1--dc23
LC record available at https://lccn.loc.gov/2018028345

Table of Contents

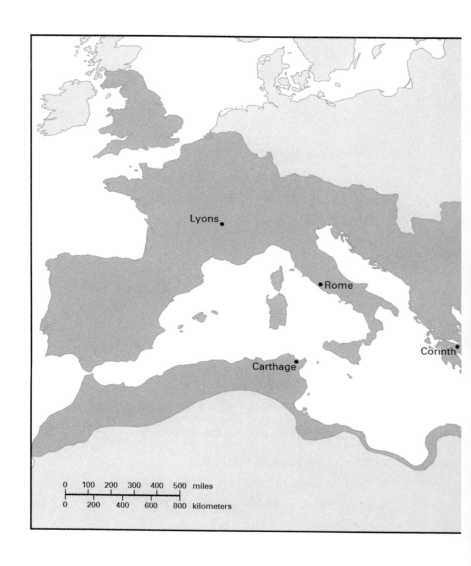

Lyons

Rome

Carthage

Corinth

| 0 | 100 | 200 | 300 | 400 | 500 | miles |
| 0 | 200 | | 400 | 600 | 800 | kilometers |

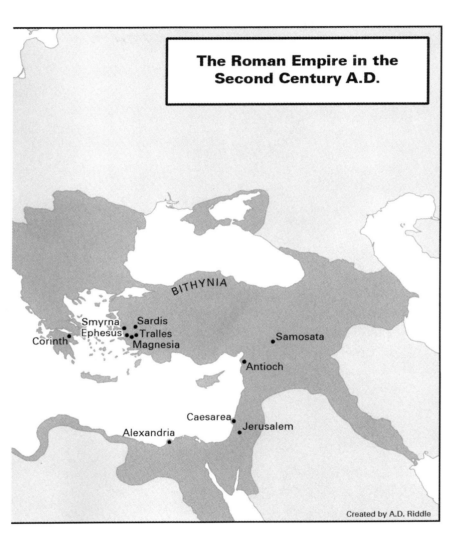

The Roman Empire in the Second Century A.D.

BITHYNIA

Smyrna
Ephesus
Corinth
Sardis
Tralles
Magnesia
Samosata
Antioch
Caesarea
Alexandria
Jerusalem

Created by A.D. Riddle

Preface

There are many books about early Christianity. Some focus in great detail on the theological development of the church, some focus on individual theologians, some focus on topics in early Christianity, and some focus on the cultural and political context for the rise of Christianity. Some of these books are intended for a learned audience, while others are intended for a general audience. Most of the authors of these books are Christians, a few are not. My first order of business, then, is to explain why we need another book on early Christianity. To do that, I am going to describe the audience I have in mind.

This is a book for the general reader who is a Christian or is interested in Christianity. While someone may encounter this book in an undergraduate classroom or pick it up and read it on their own, the audience I have in mind is adults who will read and discuss this in community: a traditional Sunday school class, a small group or home group, or a reading group. This goes a long way to explain the format of the book.

There are fifteen short chapters in this book, and these chapters move chronologically through early Christianity from about AD 100 to 300. The chapters are grouped into three parts, and each part addresses a general question about the early church: (1) what was Christianity like around the year AD 100? (2) How did Christians respond to persecution in the Roman World? and (3) How did early Christians deepen their faith and cultivate a spiritual life in the midst of their hostile world? Each chapter concludes with questions that are intended as springboards for discussion and a bridge between Christians in the Roman Empire and the lived experience of Christians today.

In short, this is a book by a Christian for Christians who would like to learn more about the early church in community with other believers. Some readers will be content with what they learn here, and that contentment would please me. Other readers might have their interest piqued by the subject of early Christianity in general or a particular topic within early Christianity. The book concludes with a "What to Read Next" section and a general bibliography that can guide further reading.

A bibliography in a book such as this also signals how dependent any scholar is on the work of colleagues and predecessors; I am no different. Here, I would also like to acknowledge a few individuals who have been helpful in this project. I am grateful to Edwin Yamauchi, a former advisor and emeritus professor of history at Miami University, for suggesting Hendrickson Publishers for this book. Both Jonathan Kline and Maggie Swofford of Hendrickson Publishers have been helpful and accommodating throughout the publishing process. A New Testament scholar and colleague at Northwestern College, John Vonder Bruegge, provided valuable insights on some of the early chapters. Finally, I am grateful to family members—John Doering, Carolyn Winn, and particularly my wife, Samantha, who read early drafts and encouraged me to write this book. Needless to say, any errors in fact or interpretation are my responsibility alone.

With a sure belief that the God of history known through Jesus Christ was on their side, Christians in the Roman Empire were finding their way in an openly hostile or, at best, disinterested world. Sometimes they demonstrated inspiring unity and courage, sometimes they took the easy path of compliance with the political and cultural forces around them, and sometimes they fought bitterly amongst themselves. They were, in other words, much like Christians today. It is my hope that you finish this book encouraged by their inspiring moments and filled with sympathetic understanding for their failings.

PART ONE

Christianity in the Year 100

Why devote an entire section of this book—five chapters—to exploring what Christianity was like at the end of the first century and beginning of the second? There are a number of good reasons for this.

First, by around AD 100 many of the New Testament books were written and circulating. While it would not be for another two centuries until the New Testament reached its final form as we know it today, by 100 Christians were already referring to the Gospels and letters of the New Testament as authoritative texts from the previous generation. By 100, in other words, the apostolic era—the period when the initial followers of Jesus were alive—was over. For the first time, a generation of Christians was in the same position in which Christians find themselves today: attempting to apply the inspired accounts of Jesus to their faith and life in the context of the older Jewish Scriptures.

Second, by AD 100, a generation had passed since the Jewish revolt against the Romans and the destruction of the Temple in Jerusalem. In the decades following the revolt, Christians thought carefully about the church's relationship with the synagogue and were developing strategies to explain their simultaneous use of the ancient Jewish Scriptures, which Christians would eventually call the Old Testament, and their rejection of Judaism. Granted, some of this had already begun in the first century, as the New Testament bears witness, but the lines between church and synagogue were becoming clearer for both sides by the turn of the first century. It is worth remembering that there is no evidence that Jewish Christians participated in any of the Jewish revolts against Rome (66–73, 115–17, 132–35), and by AD 100 a statement against Christians had become part of the order of service in the synagogue. The "parting of the ways," as scholars sometimes call the separation between Judaism and Christianity, was well under way by the year 100.

Third, for the decades spanning roughly AD 95 to 130, we have a rich collection of texts commonly known as the "apostolic fathers." These writings are valuable witnesses to how Christians were thinking about God and themselves as God's people in the Roman Empire. As the following chapters make clear, we learn a number of things from them: how Christians thought about Jesus, how Christians worshiped, how they understood the Bible, and on what points they disagreed with each other. We will be using these texts, then, as our guide to try to answer this question: What was Christianity like in year 100?

IMPORTANT DATES

Emperor Augustus: r. 27 BC–AD 14	First Letter of Clement of Rome: 97–98
Crucifixion of Jesus: 33	Emperor Trajan: r. 98–117
Emperor Nero: r. 54–68	Ignatius of Antioch martyred: 110?
Persecution of Nero: 64?	Pliny governor of Bithynia: 111–13
First Jewish revolt: 66–73	Second Jewish revolt: 115–17
Temple destroyed: 70	Tacitus writes the Annals: 116–20
Emperor Domitian: r. 81–96	Third Jewish revolt: 132–35

Christians, Jews, and Romans in the First Century

Rome had been a power in the Mediterranean world for centuries when Jesus was born, but the Roman Empire, as it would exist for centuries after Jesus died, came into its own during the life of Jesus. An older contemporary of Jesus, Octavian Caesar (reigned 27 BC–AD 14), or Augustus Caesar, was the first Roman emperor and in his own time was understood to have ushered in a new era in Roman history. In fact, Augustus claimed as much through his own propaganda. On coins issued during his reign, Augustus was stylized as the restorer of Rome, the one who would bring peace and prosperity after decades of civil war. Perhaps most strikingly, Augustus insisted that people think of him as a ruler associated with the gods, and on his coins Augustus is regularly referred to as "son of god." Just how far this had become the party-line of the Roman governing class is apparent in a public inscription from Priene, an ancient city located in what is now the western coast of Turkey. In this inscription, the local authorities recognized Augustus as the "the savior" and further claimed that "the birthday of the god [Augustus] was the beginning of the gospel for the world."[1]

Although not all the successors of Augustus in the early first century had his political skills or success, the Roman governing class nevertheless remained confident that they were ruling by divine right over the Mediterranean world. It was difficult for those they governed to argue with the military and political success of the Romans and suicidal to challenge it. They dominated the Mediterranean basin and the surrounding areas: from England to Portugal to North Africa to Iraq and to the Danube and Rhine valleys.

Just how dangerous it was for anyone to contest Roman power is evident in the tragic history of the first-century Jewish revolt.

First-century Judaism within the context of the Roman imperial system was a complicated interconnection of religion, politics, and history. Early Christian texts of the New Testament as well as Jewish sources from this period reflect this complexity. Many Jews expected and longed for God's anointed servant, the Messiah, to come and lead the Jewish people to freedom and prosperity, and some had even become violent in their desire to overthrow Rome.

This perfect storm of theological, social, and political forces exploded in the Jewish revolt of AD 66–73. At first successful against the Romans, the hopelessly divided and eventually out-manned Jewish forces were defeated and the Romans made an example of the Jewish people, their city, and their holy places. Jerusalem was significantly damaged and the temple was destroyed. Some Jews fled; many died. How much the Romans actually understood about Jewish belief and practice is uncertain, but what most Romans concluded, undoubtedly, was that the Jewish people had strange religious ideas and were politically dangerous. This danger to the peace and stability of the empire would have been driven home to the next generation of Roman elites when the Jews rebelled a second time during the emperor Trajan's campaign in Mesopotamia in 115, and then a third and last time in 132. In fact, it is reasonable to conclude with historian W. H. C. Frend that the deviant religion that the Roman elites viewed as dangerous in the early second century was not Christianity but Judaism.[2]

This not to say that Christianity was treated benignly or passed unscathed through the first-century Roman Mediterranean world; on the contrary, Christians at the turn of the first century had good reason to be skittish about their position because of the suffering of their early leaders. Jesus, a Palestinian Jew learned in the Scriptures, was rejected by much of the Jewish community as a false prophet and executed by the Roman authorities. Paul—another learned Jew, Roman citizen, and early Christian—believed that Judaism was fulfilled in the person of the Lord Jesus and that this was the gospel, the good news, for all people in the Roman Empire, Jew and non-Jew alike. He too was executed by the Roman authorities, and other early followers of Jesus experienced similar fates.

Writings about Jesus by Paul and other first century Christians by the turn of the first century were already circulating as a new body of authoritative texts we call the "New Testament" today. These writings took their place alongside the Scriptures, a collection of texts from the ancient Israelites originally written in Hebrew and known to early Christians in a Greek translation, which we call the "Old Testament" today. Traditional Jews and Christians, members of both the synagogue and the church throughout the Mediterranean world, affirmed the authority of the Scriptures. Rather than uniting the two groups, however, this only divided them. Christians developed their own different interpretation of the Scriptures in no small part because they, and not Jews, accepted the new writings on Jesus as authoritative texts alongside the Scriptures. The letters of Paul and other writings functioned, in the minds of Christians, as the answer key for truly understanding the Scriptures. Both the Old and New Testaments convinced Christians that they were not of the world around them and encouraged them to maintain an uneasy relationship with the dominant cultural and political order.

If we want to understand this worldview of the Christians at the end of the first century, then we must start with what they would have learned from the Bible. Three items in particular are worth stressing here.

First, and not surprisingly, these texts overwhelmingly reveal that Jesus is Lord (a title of divine authority), that he is the Son of God, that he is the Christ (God's anointed one), and that he is the Savior whose resurrection from the dead has brought salvation to all who have faith in him. These truths constitute what early Christians regularly called the gospel or the good news in these documents. There can be no doubt that scholars are right about just how provocative Christians were being when they made these claims. It was not Augustus and his successors who were the saviors and divinely appointed rulers and sons of God. In the view of Christians, the Roman imperial party-line was decidedly not "good news." Christians publicly declared a different gospel.

Second, it is obvious to anyone who reads the New Testament that while there was an order to Christian communities complete with an authority structure and moral guidelines, there were also strong disagreements among Christians. One source of this disagreement seems to come from those who wished Christianity to remain strongly connected to ancient Jewish belief and practice. One can see this playing out in Acts 15 and in Paul's letter to the Galatians. A second source of this disagreement arose from those who came into the church without any background at all in Judaism and who were not interested in following the moral code of Judaism. Paul's letters, particularly the Corinthian correspondence, reveal this controversy. As we will see in what follows, Paul's letters documenting disagreements among Christians in the mid first century spoke directly to Christians living in the year 100 who faced similar challenges in their own churches.

Third, early Christians believed with good reason that they were up against a hostile world. The Gospels reveal that a collusion of Roman imperial officials and a leading faction within Judaism led to the crucifixion of Jesus, while Paul's letters and the Acts of the apostles bear witness that there was consistent pressure on the church in the first few decades after Jesus' death. Just as important, however, is the evidence in the book of Revelation. However we might wish to interpret this apocalyptic text—Christians have certainly differed over the centuries on how to interpret it—it certainly assumes a political order intent on destroying the church.

Apart from the persecutions recorded in the New Testament, there are two instances during the first century that could have contributed to this mindset. In the 60s, prior to the outbreak of the Jewish revolt, the emperor Nero (r. 54–68) persecuted Christians in Rome, and during the reign of Domitian (r. 81–96) some Christians were persecuted as well.

According to the Roman historian Tacitus, Nero attempted to shift the blame from himself to the Christians for a destructive fire in Rome and, as more and more were rounded up, found them guilty "not so much of firing the city as of hatred against mankind."[3] Tacitus was no fan of Christianity; in fact, he regarded it as a "mischievous superstition" characterized by "abominations."[4] He was also not a fan of Nero, and he reports that the emperor's cruelty toward the Christians garnered sympathy for them among the Roman people while increasing their loathing of the emperor. It is important to note that this was not an empire-wide persecution (it was confined to the city of Rome) and, as Tacitus clearly indicates, the impetus was not so much an attack on Christians for their beliefs as a manifestation of Nero's cowardice and cruelty toward a population he could easily scape-goat.

Christian authors writing a century or more after the event claimed that the emperor Domitian also initiated a persecution against Christians.[5] Although no Roman author mentions a persecution of Christians, they do document Domitian's zeal against the Jews who were lax in paying the financial penalty required after the Romans ended the Jewish revolt.[6] It is possible that a few Christians suffered—largely because many Christians were Jewish—but, as in the case of Nero, this does not seem to have been a persecution honed to attack the church. The book of Revelation in the New Testament, though grounded in the memory of the persecution of Nero, was probably completed in the context of Domitian's reign and reflects the difficult position of some Christians because of Domitian's antagonism toward the Jews.

Over the course of this book, we will return to these three issues that were prominent in the New Testament and problematic to Christians living in the Roman world: what Christians thought about the person and work of Jesus, how Christians dealt with internal disunity, and how Christians responded to the sometimes hostile Roman establishment.

To conclude this chapter, we will listen in on one Roman official determining how to deal with Christians in the early second century. Pliny [PLIN-ee] the Younger, a contemporary of the historian Tacitus, was the governor of Bithynia in north central Turkey from 111 to 113.[7] During the year he was in this position, he often wrote letters to the emperor at the time, Trajan, for advice or to report on his activities. In one of these letters, Pliny wrote to the emperor seeking approval for how he had handled an outbreak of accusations against Christians in his province. After his investigation, he informed Trajan what he had learned about these Christians:

They maintained, however, that all that their guilt or error involved was that they were accustomed to assemble at dawn on a fixed day, to sing a hymn antiphonally to Christ as God, and to bind themselves by an oath, not for the commission of some crime, but to avoid acts of theft, brigandage, and adultery, not to break their word, and not to withhold money deposited with them when asked for it. When these rites were completed, it was their custom to depart, and then to assemble again to take food, which was however common and harmless. They had ceased, they said, to do this following my edict, by which in accordance with your instructions I had outlawed the existence of secret brotherhoods. So I thought it all the more necessary to ascertain the truth from two maidservants, who were called deaconesses, even by employing torture. I found nothing other than a debased and boundless superstition.[8]

Pliny, like Tacitus, found Christianity appalling. He too used the word superstition, highlighting it by labeling it "boundless" and "debased," and he too was convinced Christians were involved in error. Even at that, one gets the sense from the letter that he was trying to figure out why exactly Christians were to be punished. Granted, their religious ideas were unusual and offensive to him, but what they were actually doing, acknowledging a god called Christ and following a strict moral code, hardly seemed to rise to a punishable offense.[9]

We will return to Pliny's letter, and Trajan's response, in Part Two of this book when we discuss persecution and martyrdom, but for the moment, there are a few things to notice about this letter. First, Pliny, like Tacitus, saw Christians as an independent group. There is no attempt here to connect Christians with Jews or identify them as a sect of Judaism. Second, this paragraph already suggests why Pliny was worried about Christians, and his worry was connected, apparently, to a directive from Trajan. The emperor was concerned about associations of all kinds throughout the empire, and he had banned other associations, such as a club dedicated to fighting fires, that hardly seem dangerous to us.[10] Pliny, a loyal Roman, was dutifully carrying out this directive and Christians end up getting caught in the dragnet. The language of the letter is fascinating as it suggests that Christians, probably aware of the political climate, had attempted to become more discrete in their gatherings. At this point, Christians would have been meeting in homes—they did not yet have church buildings—but one wonders, how public their gatherings had been before the crackdown on associations began.

Third, for all that, Pliny was struggling to find a reason to condemn Christians. One is reminded of Pontius Pilate, who, according to the Gospels, was convinced that Jesus' actions did not merit punishment but who also wanted to maintain order in Jerusalem. Pliny knew he was not the first Roman official to encounter Christians, but he also freely admitted his own ignorance at the outset of the letter: "I have never been present at an examination of Christians. I do not know what punishment is required or how far it is to be carried out."[11] One can sense his desperation in the final two sentences of the paragraph I quoted on the previous page. He simply had to get to the bottom of this once and for all. His choice, torturing two slave women who were also leaders among the Christians, seems cruel, but in Roman thinking this was completely reasonable. Under Roman law, the testimony of slaves was only accepted under torture because everyone assumed that slaves would only tell the truth when in extreme pain.[12] Perhaps he was relieved to find that Christians were not involved in political subversion, but he was also no closer to a good answer to his questions on what to do with people who were seemingly harmless, and surprisingly moral, but who had religious ideas that were socially unsettling.

As it turns out, Pliny was an acute observer of the church. What he identified as the essential elements to the Christian identity—a commitment to Christ as Lord and a moral way of life—is present everywhere in Christian writings from around the year 100. In the following chapters, we will look at several examples of how Christian authors expressed this.

DISCUSSION QUESTIONS

*1. Why would the Christian proclamation of "the gospel"
have been seen as subversive and dangerous to Roman officials? In what ways could the gospel be seen as subversive and
dangerous today?*

*2. Winn claims there are three basic things early Christians
would have understood from the Bible: Jesus Christ is Lord,
Son of God, and Savior; Christian communities have a necessary order and structure; Christians will face persecution. Are
there other major themes from the Bible that you would add to
this list?*

*3. A busy and disinterested outsider, Pliny made a quick
assessment of Christians: they worship Jesus and have a moral
code. What would a busy outsider conclude about Christians
today? Is there a difference between what Christians might
hope they would conclude and what people might actually
conclude about Christians?*

CHAPTER 2

A New Way of Life: *Didache* and *The Epistle of Barnabas*

The last chapter concluded with a discussion of the Roman governor Pliny the Younger. As you recall, he was confronted with the task of figuring out what to do with Christians. What struck him was not so much their religious beliefs, though he did dutifully note that they worshiped a god named Christ, but their way of life, which was hardly criminal. Christians, he commented, bound "themselves by oath, not to some crime, but not to commit fraud, theft, or adultery, not falsify their trust, nor to refuse to return a trust when called upon to do so."[1] As far as he could see, if Christians were to be found guilty, it would not be for breaking the law; in fact, Pliny seems impressed that Christians adhered to a remarkably moral life.

The writings of Christians from the time of Pliny tell us that he was an astute observer of the fledgling church. At the turn of the first century, Christians took seriously the idea that a peculiar "way of life" was essential to their religious identity.

"There are two ways, one of life and one of death, and there is a great difference between these two ways."[2] With these words, one of the most intriguing Christian documents from the period AD 70–130 begins. The full title, "The Teaching of the Lord to the Gentiles through the Twelve Apostles," is rarely used; instead, it has become common to refer to this text from the word "Teaching" in the original Greek: *Didache* [DID-uh-kay]. This text, claiming to summarize the teachings of all the apostles, bears all the marks of being an edited document, and the author or authors are unknown. It probably reached the form in which we have it by the end of our period (c. 130) but contains material that dates from much earlier, perhaps from the time of the apostles.

There are two main parts to this text. The first part comprises a description of the "two ways," referenced above, and the second provides an account of early Christian liturgy and church order. In many ways, the *Didache* is a handbook for those wishing to join the church. First, the seekers learn what the Christian way of life is like and then, if they are still interested, they learn about baptism, the regular practice of Christian worship, and the leaders of the community.[3] There is no presentation of Christian theology or the gospel in this text, presumably because the author assumes he is writing for an audience of people who have already been convinced about the work and person of Jesus and are ready to fully commit to the church.

The "two ways" teaching, our topic for this chapter, presents what one can expect in the life of a Christian and the life of a non-Christian. It assumes no overlap and no confusion of categories; a person is either one thing or the other. The *Didache* is not the only place we find this in Christian literature from the period. A shorter version of what appears in the *Didache* is found in the so-called *Epistle of Barnabas*, which we will discuss at the end of this chapter, and a variation on this same concern for a Christian way of life is found in the first letter of Clement of Rome (see chapter three). It is likely that Christians adapted the "two ways" teaching from Jewish methods of moral instruction, ultimately rooted in the Law and the wisdom literature of the Old Testament.[4]

Immediately after introducing the two ways, as quoted above, the *Didache* continues by clarifying what marks the Christian: "Now this is the way of life: first, you shall love God who made you. Second, you shall love your neighbor as yourself; but whatever you do not wish to happen to you, do not do to another."[5] The great commandment and the golden rule are the foundation for this way of life, and what follows is a lengthy description of other passages of Scripture that expand on these two principles. Some of these are drawn directly from the Gospels (particularly Matthew), others are extensions of Jesus' teachings, and still others are drawn from the Ten Commandments. The following is an example of how the author would combine these sources:

The second commandment of the teaching is: You shall not mur-
der; you shall not commit adultery; you shall not corrupt children;
you shall not be sexually immoral; you shall not steal; you shall
not practice magic; you shall not engage in sorcery; you shall
not abort a child or commit infanticide. You shall not covet your
neighbor's possessions; you shall not commit perjury; you shall not
give false testimony; you shall not speak evil; you shall not hold
a grudge. You shall not be double-minded or double-tongued, for
the double tongue is a deadly snare. Your word must not be false
or meaningless, but confirmed by action. You shall not be greedy
or avaricious, or a hypocrite or malicious or arrogant. You shall
not hatch evil plots against your neighbor. You shall not hate any-
one; instead you shall reprove some, and pray for some, and some
you shall love more than your own life.[6]

Those who know the Bible will immediately recognize that this
passage contains a medley of the Ten Commandments, other Old
Testament laws, and teachings from the New Testament. There are
also practices related to the culture of the Roman Mediterranean
world that are presented here as unacceptable for a Christian way
of life. In fact, in this passage we have two clusters of prohibitions,
and the organizational logic of the passage depends on the Ten
Commandments. The first cluster is based on commandments five
through seven—do not murder, do not commit adultery, do not
steal—while the second cluster is sequenced around the last two
commandments—do not bear false witness and do not covet.

   What is immediately noteworthy to a modern reader in the first
cluster are the prohibitions against pederasty (do not corrupt children), magic and sorcery, abortion, and infanticide. In part, what
the author is doing here is showing how the biblical commands
apply to practices that are not specifically condemned in the Ten
Commandments. Thus, the Christian sexual ethic built around
marital fidelity excludes not only fornication (literally sex with a
prostitute, but more broadly, as is translated here, sexual immorality) but also pederasty, a common practice in the Greco-Roman
world.[7] Similarly, the author has deliberately structured this passage
so that the command against murder frames it. The commandment

is clear enough, but the author clarifies that this includes infants
born and unborn, and that the all too common practice in antiquity
of infanticide and abortion are not to be part of the Christian life.
From there, the author brings up the command against theft and
then the bit about magic that, to modern ears, seems out of place.
It would not have seemed odd to people living in the Roman Mediterranean. Sorcery in the ancient world often referred to the use of
special ingredients, particular items, and supposed magical words
to harm someone or gain the romantic affection of someone you
wanted. It could also refer to the use of special ingredients as a poi-
son or to produce an abortion.[8] The ancient audience would have
grasped immediately that magic was related to all three prohibitions and understood why magic could not be part of the Christian
way of life.

In the second cluster of prohibitions, the final two commandments are restated in several different ways in order to drive them
home. Do not speak evil or commit perjury, do not hold a grudge,
do not be double-minded or double-tongued, and follow through
on your word with action all are produced or arise from dishonesty.
Further, avoiding covetousness involves not only curbing greed, but
also hypocrisy and arrogance. The central failure in all these cases,
and in fact for the entire passage, is what he identifies at the end:
"You shall not hate anyone."[9] Hatred is the root problem behind dis-
regarding all these commands and ought not to mark the Christian
way of life, a life that, as he already established, should manifest love
for God and neighbor.

The author returns to some of these same points a few paragraphs later and, through the repetition, reveals that what is most
concerning is the real danger of magic, dishonesty, and a hateful
spirit.

> My child, do not be an augur, since it leads to idolatry. Do not be
> an enchanter or an astrologer or a magician, or even desire to see
> them, for all these things breed idolatry. My child, do not be a liar,
> since lying leads to theft. Do not be avaricious or conceited, for
> all these things breed thefts. My child, do not be a grumbler, since

it leads to blasphemy. Do not be arrogant or evil-minded, for all
these things breed blasphemies.[10]

Avoiding sorcery, maintaining personal integrity, and avoiding the kind of misanthropic behavior that leads to blasphemy (i.e.
outsiders observing the words and deeds of Christians and speaking ill against them and their God) concern the author, but there
are other items that the author stresses in this section. The *Didache*
assumes that many readers are following the normal activities of
human existence: they are marrying, having children, and manag-
ing households. As with everything else, there is a Christian way
to do this as well:

> *You shall not withhold your hand from your son or your daughter,*
> *but from their youth you shall teach them the fear of God. You*
> *shall not give orders to your male slave or female servant (who*
> *hope in the same God as you do) when you are angry, lest they*
> *cease to fear the God who is over you both. For he comes to call*
> *not with regard to reputation but those whom the Spirit has*
> *prepared. And you slaves shall be submissive to your masters in*
> *respect and fear, as to a symbol of God.*[11]

Beyond their relationships within their homes, the author also
comments on their relationships within the church. First of all, they
should regularly be committed to their fellow believers: "Moreover, you shall seek out daily the presence of the saints, so that you
might find support in their words. You shall not cause divisions, but
you shall make peace between those who quarrel."[12] Second, they
should be generous. "You shall not hesitate to give, nor shall you
grumble when giving, for you will know who is the good paymaster of the reward. You shall not turn away from someone in need,
but shall share everything with your brother or sister, and do not
claim that anything is your own."[13] By stating what they should
do and what they should avoid, therefore, the author is detailing
what he began with: the Christian way of life is founded on a consistent love of God and love of neighbor. Does this mean that the
author expects perfection from all those who would identify with

the church and with Christ through baptism? One might begin to think so, except that at the end of his description on the way of life, he allows and assumes that Christians will not always live up to these standards. "In church you shall confess your transgressions, and you shall not approach your prayer with an evil conscience. This is the way of life."[14]

What follows, then, are the actions that consistently characterize those who pursue the "way of death." It is a much more condensed list, containing many of the things the author had already condemned in the description of the Christian way of life, including sexual immorality, sorcery, duplicity, and avarice along with a repetition of things forbidden in the Ten Commandments. In addition, we have an explicit condemnation of greed that throws into sharper relief the kind of generosity he expects from Christians. Those on the way of death, he explains, "love worthless things, pursue reward, have no mercy for the poor, do not work on behalf of the oppressed, do not know the one who made them, are murderers of children, corrupters of God's creation, who turn away from someone in need, who oppress the afflicted . . ."[15] Though these are normally characteristic of those outside the Church and Christ, the author recognizes that it is possible to stray from the Christian way of life. He concludes, "May you be delivered, children, from all these things!"[16]

To demonstrate just how pervasive this kind of thinking was among Christians around AD 100, we will look quickly at *The Epistle of Barnabas*. The Barnabas of the New Testament is not the author, though the unknown author may have been communicating what was believed to be the teaching of Barnabas. Among the topics the author discusses is a brief "two ways" teaching that differentiates between the "way of light" and the "way of darkness." Pseudo-Barnabas, as the author is sometimes called, begins by insisting that the reader love God and "glorify him who redeemed you from death"; not be sexually immoral, commit adultery, or corrupt children; and love their neighbors and therefore "not abort a child nor, again, commit infanticide."[17] Further, the author tells them, "You must not withhold your hand from your son or your daughter, but from their youth shall teach them the fear of God."[18] They should "not be double-minded or double-tongued," "share everything" with their neighbors, and claim nothing as their own.[19] The author insists on generosity: "You shall not hesitate to give, nor shall you grumble when giving, but you will know who is the good paymaster of the reward."[20] Finally the writer insists that they remain united: "you shall not cause division, but shall make peace between those who quarrel by bringing them together."[21] Similarly, *The Epistle of Barnabas* echoes what the *Didache* says about the way of death or, in this letter, the "way of darkness." Those pursuing this way exhibit recognizable characteristics: idolatry, sexual immorality, avarice, duplicity, arrogance, and sorcery. They "love worthless things, pursue reward, have no mercy for the poor, do not work on behalf of the oppressed." Further, they are "reckless with slander, do not know the one who made them, are murderers of children, corrupters of God's creation, who turn away from someone in need, who oppress the afflicted."[22]

The similarities between the *Didache* and *The Epistle of Barnabas* are remarkable and some of the sections are exact duplicates of each other. Given that both of these documents originate around the same time, it is unlikely that one was dependent on the other; rather, both are drawing on an older common tradition that circulated widely among Christian communities in the first century. Christians living around the year 100 understood that a life based on the biblical commands to love God and their neighbors was essential to their identity, and this identity would differentiate them sharply from the cultural norms around them. In the next chapter we will see how another writer from this period, Clement of Rome, similarly confirms Pliny's observation that Christians were committed to Christ and a particular way of life.

DISCUSSION QUESTIONS

1. The "two ways" teaching depicts an ideal Christian way of life. What seems to have been the most important features of this way of life? Are these things still important for Christians today? What would you emphasize as being essential to a Christian way of life?

2. Over and over again in the New Testament and early Christian writings of the first few centuries authors warn against using magic. Why was magic a problem for the author of the Didache? *Most people today in the western world are not tempted to use magic. Has technology replaced magic for Western people and, if so, does it pose a danger to Christians similar to magic in the ancient world?*

3. The author of the Didache *and* The Epistle of Barnabas *show how the Ten Commandments and the teachings of Jesus apply to their time and place. If you were to rewrite the section from the* Didache *quoted above for your time and place, what would you include?*

CHAPTER 3

Clement of Rome
and the Church of Corinth

1 Clement, named after its author, is the oldest Christian document outside the New Testament that has survived. Clement was an elder or bishop (as we will see in a moment, these words were apparently synonyms for him) among the Christians in the city of Rome. His letter, addressed to the Christians in Corinth, begins by noting that it is late: "Because of the sudden and repeated misfortunes and reverses which have happened to us, brothers, we acknowledge that we have been somewhat slow in giving attention to the matters in dispute among you."[1] It is likely that the reason for the delay was the extent to which the church in Rome was thrown into disarray by Domitian's erratic attacks on Jews and, by extension, some Christians.[2] We should be thankful that he did get around to writing the letter, because of what it reveals about how Christians in one city thought about an argument going on among Christians in another city.

Clement's first move in the letter is a smart one: he reminds his Corinthian audience that they share a religious common ground, the "glorious and holy rule of our tradition."[3] Just to be sure they understand, he briefly reviews the contents of this holy rule at the outset of the letter. The foundation of their shared faith is their common belief that the blood of Christ brings salvation from the Father to all who repent.[4] Throughout the letter he returns to elements of this common faith.

First, the Christians in Rome and Corinth share a common belief in the "gospel" about the Lord Jesus Christ, who "was sent forth from God."[5] In his letter, Clement closely associates Jesus with God, uses the title Lord (a divine title) for him repeatedly, and uses other language to suggest that Jesus is fully divine. He is, for example, the "the majestic scepter of God" and the "high priest."[6] Christ is also the final and full sacrifice, whose blood was offered for the redemption of all who believe in him. Toward the end of the letter, Clement writes: "Because of the love he had for us, and in accordance with God's will, Jesus Christ our Lord gave his blood for us, his flesh for our flesh, and his life for our lives."[7] Clement assumes that Christians in Rome and Corinth share a common Christology—a set of beliefs about who Jesus is—that views Christ as fully divine and also fully human, complete with flesh, blood, and soul. As we will see, this union of Christ's humanity and divinity in one person will form part of his argument for unity among the Corinthians. Similarly, Clement also assumes that his audience shares a Trinitarian understanding of God with the church in Rome. He advises the Christians in Corinth to continue "trusting in his most holy and majestic name" and to remember that their salvation is certain "as God lives, and the Lord Jesus Christ lives and the Holy Spirit."[8]

Second, he assumes that Christians in Corinth, like Christians in Rome, accept the authority of Scripture. Clement's letter, which is reminiscent of some of Paul's letters and the New Testament book "Hebrews," is full of quotations and allusions to the Old Testament. In this letter, Clement primarily uses the Old Testament as a series of examples for the Christians in Corinth. Most of these examples are positive; Abraham, Moses, Job, Rahab, David, Elijah, Elisha, and Ezekiel are among those he discusses. A few, however, are negative examples: Cain, the Egyptians at the time of the Exodus, and Saul. His normal practice is to quote extensively from a biblical passage and then comment on how the passage applies to their situation. He saw no need for elaborate methods of exegesis; the texts of the Old Testament, inspired by the Holy Spirit, speak directly to the Christians in Rome and Corinth. Though not nearly as frequently, Clement's letter also draws on New Testament books. Unsurprisingly, the most prominent are Paul's letters to the Corinthians; however, he uses other letters of Paul as well. Twice Clement makes allusions to passages from the Gospels, but in both cases it is impossible to determine from which gospel he is quoting. His method is to invite his audience to "remember the words of the Lord Jesus," and then recount these words in a way that suggests he is quoting verbatim but whose text does not correspond exactly to any passage in the four Gospels as we know them.[9]

Drawing on these two shared assumptions—the centrality of Jesus as Savior and the authority of Scripture—Clement has two agenda items for this letter: encouraging Christians in Corinth to restore harmony and peace among themselves and reminding them to maintain the high standards of a Christian way of life. These, in his mind, are the two primary and defining characteristics of the church.

From the outset of the letter, Clement makes it clear that he is addressing "the detestable and unholy schism" that has divided the Corinthian church.[10] Clement reminds them of the tragic nature of this schism and how the church in Corinth was formerly known for its faith, piety, hospitality, humility, obedience to God's laws, and respect for authority. At one time, the church was characterized by the self-discipline of the young people, the blameless women who managed their homes with discretion, the zeal of all to remember the words of Christ in their hearts, the abundant presence of the Holy Spirit among them, and the fervency of their prayers.[11] Now, however, the Corinthians are characterized by "jealousy and envy" and "strife and sedition." On this, Clement writes, "For this reason, righteousness and peace stand at a distance, while each one has abandoned the fear of God and become nearly blind with respect to faith in him, neither walking according to the laws of his commandments nor living in accordance with his duty to Christ."[12]

At the beginning of this letter, then, Clement is confronting the Corinthian Christians with their failure to maintain unity, but he is also showing that peaceful harmony and a proper Christian way of life are causally linked. Schism and a breakdown of morality always accompany each other; in the case of the Corinthians, their rebellion against the pastoral authority of the church also suggested a complete collapse of Christian morality.

For Clement, harmony and peace among Christians primarily means living in respectful obedience to those whom God has seen fit to place in positions of authority in the church. Just as he did with the ancient Israelites, God has continued to command his people to bring offerings and participate in ceremonies at certain times and in certain places under the authority of certain individuals. Engaging in separatist gatherings for Christian worship does not signal a group living according to God's expectation for humility and obedience; those who do this are not under the authority of Christ. Unity, then, for Clement, is about proper order and proper authority which, toward the end of his letter, he defines clearly.

> The apostles received the gospel for us from the Lord Jesus Christ; Jesus, the Christ, was sent forth from God. So then, Christ is from God, and the apostles are from Christ. Both, therefore, came of the will of God in good order. Having therefore received their orders and being fully assured by the resurrection of our Lord Jesus Christ and full of faith in the word of God, they went forth with the firm assurance that the Holy Spirit gives, preaching the good news that God's Kingdom was about to come. So, preaching both in the country and in the towns, they appointed their first fruits, when they had tested them by the Spirit, to be bishops and deacons for future believers.[13]

After reflecting on the relevance of the Old Testament law for the choice of priests and the problems that could occur and concluding that Moses already spoke on this matter, Clement picks up his reasoning and returns to the situation in Corinth.

> Our apostles likewise knew, through our Lord Jesus Christ, that there would be strife over the bishop's office. For this reason, therefore, having received complete foreknowledge, they appointed the leaders mentioned earlier and afterwards they gave the offices a permanent character; that is, if they should die, other approved men should succeed to their ministry. These, therefore, who were appointed by them or, later on, by other reputable men with the consent of the whole church, and who have ministered to the flock of Christ blamelessly, humbly, peaceable, and unselfishly, and for a long time have been well-spoken of by all—these we consider to be unjustly removed from their ministry.[14]

The revolt of the Corinthian Christians against their elders and bishops (Clement uses these terms interchangeably) resulted in a situation where their very salvation is in question. The true people of God have never rebelled against their leaders; those who did this in the past were "[a]bominable people, full of all wickedness, who were stirred up to such a pitch of wrath that they tortured cruelly those who served God with holy and blameless resolve."[15] Not only does the divisiveness of the church of Corinth throw into question whether the rebels are even Christians, it also made the church a subject of ridicule among non-Christians. Clement is particularly harsh with them on this point: "you heap blasphemies upon the name of the Lord because of your stupidity."[16]

The solution is harmony and peace. Harmony, Clement explains, is written into the created order, and just as God created harmony in the physical world, so he expects his people to maintain such an orderly harmony in the church.[17] Maintaining harmony means recognizing one's own rank and, with humility, maintaining this proper order. Similarly, the Corinthians should honor and cling to those who "devoutly practice peace." Along with harmony, the importance of peace among Christians is a constant refrain in this letter.[18]

At its heart, Clement's letter is a call to Christian virtue. Based on the life and work of Jesus and based on the authority of Scripture, Clement insists that the Christians of Corinth repent and return to the life of virtue that used to characterize them. Why should they do this? Not, Clement is clear, because they will merit God's favor through virtue. Just as the tribe of Levi's priests received great honor simply because it was God's will and not because they in any way deserved this honor, so too should Christians not attempt to win status with God.

> And so we, having been called through his will in Christ Jesus, are not justified through ourselves or through our own wisdom or understanding or piety, or works that we have done in holiness of heart, but through faith, by which the Almighty God has justified all who have existed from the beginning. . . . What then shall we

do, brothers? Shall we idly abstain from doing good, and forsake love? May the Master never allow this to happen, at least to us; but let us hasten with earnestness and zeal to accomplish every good work.[19]

The virtues he emphasizes at the beginning of the letter, which he calls the "way of truth" that is in "harmony with his faultless will," are love and humility.[20] Both of these virtues will ensure the presence of peace and harmony among them. Both virtues will also foster in them all the other virtues the Corinthians had once demonstrated.

Clement's letter to the church in Corinth represents the Christian viewpoint of one city in the year 97, but it is nevertheless striking how well it accords with what we have already read about other Christians at the turn of the first century. His call for the Corinthians to follow a "way of truth" should remind us of the "two ways" teaching that characterized much of the thinking about the church's identity around the year 100. In the *Didache* and *The Epistle of Barnabas*, as you recall, the "two ways" teaching was a detailed summary of specific virtues that ought to characterize a Christian's life along with prohibitions against particular vices drawn from the Old Testament and the Sermon on the Mount. While Clement does not provide a detailed description of such a life, it is clear that he has two contrasting ways of life in mind and is concerned that the Corinthian Christians have strayed too far from the right way.

Elite Romans—such as Pliny or Tacitus—identified Christians as followers of a pernicious or mischievous superstition, never as violent insurrectionists.[21] This may be why Clement was so agitated at the Christians in Corinth. Any hint of unrest among Christians might lead to assumptions that, like the Jews, they were dangerous. The observations of Pliny, at any event, are once again affirmed by Clement's letter. For Clement and for the Roman church, the heart of Christian identity was devotion to the Lord Jesus Christ, the Savior, and a harmonious unity among Christians based around love, humility, and a moral way of life. While it is a letter idiosyncratic to a particular place and time, Clement's words reflect a shared vision of how Christians thought about themselves and their common life in the Roman Mediterranean.

In the next chapter, we will listen in on another Christian letter writer who was an exact contemporary of Pliny and Tacitus and whose letters to the churches help us understand further the nature of Christianity in the year 100.

DISCUSSION QUESTIONS

1. *What is the common faith that Christians in Rome and Corinth share and why does Clement think this is important?*

2. *Why were harmony, peace, and unity so essential to Clement? Is there anything that could require Christians to separate from each other?*

3. *Winn concludes by noting that Clement's letter is similar to the* Didache *and* The Epistle of Barnabas. *Based on what you have read, how is* 1 Clement *similar to or different from these other texts?*

CHAPTER 4

Ignatius of Antioch and True Christianity

At some point during the reign of Emperor Trajan (r. 98–117), the same emperor to whom Pliny wrote his letter about interrogating Christians, Ignatius [ig-NAY-shus], the bishop of the Christians of Antioch, was arrested, taken to Rome, and martyred. As he was making the long journey from Antioch to Rome, Ignatius wrote letters to churches along the route, including some churches that Paul had founded and to whom he addressed letters. In his letters, Ignatius communicates his suspicion that he will die in the arena as a victim of the games. Later accounts confirm that this is what happened to him.

Like Clement of Rome, Ignatius was concerned about the unity of the churches to which he wrote and, just as Clement, believed that unity means living in submission to the leaders of the church. For Ignatius, this concern about unity is directly linked to his concern about heresy because in his mind unity around church leadership is the best way to stave off the threat of heresy entering the church. In this chapter, we will look at how he understood Christian unity and why he was so concerned about heresy entering the church.

To begin, we need to understand the leadership structure Ignatius assumes to be the norm. Remember that for Clement of Rome, elders and bishops are terms for the same leadership position. Ignatius also speaks about elders and bishops, but he considers their positions to be separate offices. In his view, the bishop is the leader of the congregation and the focal point for church unity, while the elders and deacons assist him.

Over and over again in these letters Ignatius stresses that Christians must unite with, respect, and obey their bishop because doing this ensures the unity of their congregation.[1] To the church in Magnesia, whose bishop was a young man, Ignatius counsels:

> Indeed it is right for you also not to take advantage of the youthfulness of your bishop, but to give him all the respect due him in accordance with the power of God the Father, just as I know the holy presbyters likewise have not taken advantage of his youthful appearance, but defer to him as one who is wise in God; yet not really to him, but to the Father of Jesus Christ, the bishop of all. . . . Be eager to do everything in godly harmony, the bishop presiding in the place of God and the presbyters in the place of the council of the apostles.[2]

To the church in Tralles Ignatius is particularly blunt: "Let everyone respect the deacons as Jesus Christ, just as they should respect the bishop, who is a model of the Father, and the presbyters as God's council and as the band of the apostles. Without these no group can be called a church."[3] For this reason, he tells the Christians in Ephesus, "It is proper for you to act together in harmony with the mind of the bishop," or, as he expresses it succinctly in his letter to the church in Philadelphia, all those who belong to God and Jesus Christ "are with the bishop."[4]

The problem, in Ignatius's view, was that there were people who were claiming to belong to Christ but were not "with the bishop." Itinerant teachers, who moved from congregation to congregation, represented an alternative leadership model that apparently some Christians preferred. Ignatius was convinced that these teachers were the prime source of false teaching. In his letters, he focuses on two areas in which these teachers were negatively influencing the churches: (1) the relationship between Judaism and Christianity and (2) the nature of Jesus as human and divine.

Ignatius was keen to clearly mark the boundaries between the church and the synagogue. In fact, Ignatius coined the word "Christianity" in opposition to the already existing word "Judaism" in order to underscore the distinction between the two groups.[5] Aware that there were Christians who wanted to blur or erase the

lines separating the two groups in Magnesia and Philadelphia, Ignatius urged the churches in both cities to maintain these boundaries.

The bishop of Magnesia was a young man, and Ignatius spends
the first half of his letter encouraging unity around this bishop.
He urges the congregation to "run together . . . to the one Jesus
Christ who came forth from the one Father."[6] The problem, he reveals immediately after this statement, is that they were not running together. Echoing some of Paul's language, Ignatius warns the
congregation:

> *Do not be deceived by strange doctrines or antiquated myths, since
> they are worthless. For if we continue to live in accordance with
> Judaism, we admit that we have not received grace. For the most
> godly prophets lived in accordance with Christ Jesus. This is why
> they were persecuted, being inspired as they were by his grace in
> order that those who are disobedient might be fully convinced
> that there is one God who revealed himself through Jesus Christ
> his Son.*[7]

Ignatius is worried about the situation in Magnesia because some
Christians—perhaps many—in the church were "living in accordance with Judaism" and following "antiquated practices." Immediately following the passage above, he makes the point that keeping
the Sabbath is one such antiquated practice that Christians have now
replaced with honoring the "Lord's Day."[8] Here, he is also confronting directly the question of whether the Old Testament Scriptures,
read in the synagogue as much as in the church, affirm Judaism
more than Christianity. Ignatius insists that this is not the case. The
"most godly prophets"—here standing for the writers of the Old
Testament—were Christians before Christ; they were "his disciples
in the Spirit."[9] Christians in Magnesia and elsewhere in the Roman
world, and not the Jews, rightly understand the Old Testament.

In his letter to the church in Philadelphia, Ignatius reveals just
how much of a debate there was over this question of how to understand the Old Testament. He begins with a warning: "If anyone ex-
pounds Judaism to you, do not listen to him." Instead, they should

only attend to those who teach "Christianity."[10] A few paragraphs later, he reveals the methods of those who expound Judaism:

> *Moreover, I urge you to do nothing in a spirit of contentiousness, but in accordance with the teaching of Christ. For I heard some people say, "If I do not find it in the archives [i.e. the Old Testament], I do not believe it in the gospel." And when I said to them "It is written," they answered me, "That is precisely the question." But for me, the "archives" are Jesus Christ, the inviolable archives are his cross and the death of his resurrection and the faith which comes through him; by these things I want, through your prayers, to be justified. The priests, too, were good, but the High Priest, entrusted with the Holy of Holies, is better; he alone has been entrusted with the hidden things of God, for he himself is the door of the Father, through which Abraham and Isaac and Jacob and the prophets and the apostles and the church enter in. All these come together in the unity of God.*[11]

The itinerant teachers "expounding Judaism" were apparently insisting that all the practices of Judaism as contained in the Old Testament were applicable to the church. Further, it would seem that these teachers were claiming a priority for the "archives" over the gospel, presumably claiming that the Old Testament has priority over the New Testament. Finally, it would appear that these teachers were claiming that salvation depends on following these practices.

Ignatius's response is to argue strongly that the heart of the archives is not a system of religious practices but rather the death and resurrection of Jesus that leads to faith and justification. Following the New Testament author of Hebrews, he makes a distinction between the priests of Israel with the true High Priest, who is the one through whom all believers over all the centuries—from Abraham down to the present—are brought "together in the unity of God."

Ignatius assumes in these letters that no bishop would either agree with these ideas or be the source of them; bishops apparently agree with him on the dangers of practicing Judaism and the dangers of itinerant teachers. The same is true with the other main concern that appears in his letters: the nature of Jesus as divine and human. While his warnings about following the practices of Judaism are localized to the two letters discussed above, this concern is present in all the letters. For Ignatius, there is no room for varying opinions about Jesus in the church. Christians must avoid all false teaching about Jesus by attending to and being united to their bishop.

Let's begin with what Ignatius declares as the proper understanding of Jesus as human and divine. In his letter to the church in Ephesus, Ignatius encourages his audience to believe "there is only one physician, who is both flesh and spirit, born and unborn, God in man, true life in death, both from Mary and from God, subject to suffering and then overcoming it, Jesus Christ our Lord."[12] Similarly, he opens his letter to the church of Smyrna by praising the "unshakeable faith" of believers who are "totally convinced with regard to our Lord that he is truly of the family of David with respect to human descent, Son of God with respect to the divine will and power, truly born of a virgin, baptized by John in order that all righteousness might be fulfilled by him, truly nailed in the flesh for us under Pontius Pilate and Herod the tetrarch."[13] Again, in the letter to the Trallians, Ignatius encourages his audience to maintain a proper understanding of Jesus, "who was of the family of David, who was the son of Mary, who really was born, who both ate and drank; who really was persecuted under Pontius Pilate, who really was crucified and died while those in heaven and on earth and under the earth looked on; who, moreover, really was raised from the dead when his Father raised him up."[14]

It is hard to miss in these passages the emphasis Ignatius places on the true humanity of Jesus that, along with his divinity, characterized his uniqueness. He stresses repeatedly the human anchors that verify his humanity: he is from the line of David, he is the son of Mary, and he was killed under Pontius Pilate. He also emphasizes his human experiences: he ate, he drank, and he had a body that was nailed to a cross. Ignatius feared that the churches to which he wrote were listening to teachers who were arguing against this.

Today, scholars refer to Ignatius's opponents as "docetists" from the Greek verb *dokeō*, "to seem or appear," because, according to Ignatius, his opponents claimed that Jesus "suffered in appearance only" and that he was not truly human.[15] It is possible that the false teachers mentioned in the New Testament book 1 John were also docetists, which explains why the elder insists on having seen and touched Jesus.[16]

Over and over, Ignatius counsels Christians to stay away from heresy. In his letter to the Trallians, he expresses it this way:

> *I urge you, therefore—yet not I, but the love of Jesus Christ—partake only of Christian food, and keep away from every strange plant, which is heresy. These people, while pretending to be trustworthy, mix Jesus Christ with themselves—like those who administer a deadly drug with honeyed wine, which the unsuspecting victim accepts without fear, and so with fatal pleasure drinks down death.*[17]

He is not sparing in his description of these teachers. They are malicious and deceitful, they are "mad dogs" and "wild beasts," and they "adulterously" corrupt faith in Christ and are justly facing the "unquenchable fire."[18] Further, they are "atheists" and "unbelievers" who are "wicked offshoots that bear deadly fruit" and "advocates of death rather than the truth."[19]

Ignatius' argument with the docetists, then, was not a friendly disagreement among believers; for him the docetists were not Christians at all and their message threatened the very existence of the church. Christians must believe that Jesus was fully human and fully divine because this faith is, in Ignatius's view, central to the identity of Christians in the Roman world. To conclude this chapter on Ignatius, we will look at two ways he expressed this link between Jesus and Christian life.

Ignatius anticipated that he would be martyred in Rome, and in his letter to the church in Rome he expresses his urgency for experiencing martyrdom. His great fear is that the Christians in Rome will attempt to rescue him through some means—potentially bribery—and rob him of this opportunity to "truly be a disciple of

Jesus Christ" by experiencing the physical pain of martyrdom.[20] What he wants, more than anything, is for the Christians of Rome to not be an obstacle to him. "Allow me to be an imitator of the suffering of my God."[21]

Ignatius' understanding of the full humanity of Christ seems to be behind such sentiments, and he makes this explicit in his letter to the church in Smyrna. False teachers who advocate docetism— "wild beasts in human form"—make the notion of martyrdom seem absurd.

> For if these things were done by our Lord in appearance only, then I am in chains in appearance only. Why, moreover, have I surrendered myself to death, to fire, to sword, or to beasts? But in any case, 'near the sword' means 'near to God'; 'with the beasts' means 'with God.' Only let it be in the name of Jesus Christ, so that I may suffer together with him! I endure everything because he himself, who is the perfect human being, empowers me.[22]

This letter makes clear that Ignatius thought his martyrdom would allow him to identify fully with Jesus' bodily human suffering. The right mindset about Jesus therefore permits Ignatius to speak of martyrdom as a path to true discipleship and a path to a true imitation of the "suffering of my God."

In this same section from the Smyrna letter where he claims that docetism invalidates martyrdom, he also points out one final way in which it makes people "contrary to the mind of God." If these false teachers are correct about Jesus, then they undermine the rationale for Christians to demonstrate love for others. His logic appears to be that if Christ did not have a body with physical needs, then there is no need to be concerned about the physical needs of others. Ignatius concludes that the docetists have "no concern for love, none for the widow, none for the orphan, none for the oppressed, none for the prisoner or the one released, none for the hungry or thirsty."[23] He expresses this same concern in a separate letter addressed to Polycarp, the bishop of the church in Smyrna, and urges him to endure as Christ endured, "who for our sake suffered, who for our sake endured in every way."[24] His fortitude as a bishop should be manifest in very practical ways.

> *Do not let widows be neglected. After the Lord, you be their guardian. . . . Do not treat slaves, whether male or female, contemptuously. . . . Flee from wicked practices; better yet, preach a sermon about them. Tell my sisters to love the Lord and to be content with their husbands physically and spiritually. In the same way command my brothers in the name of Jesus Christ to love their wives, as the Lord loves the church.*[25]

Ignatius believed that love for neighbor must mark a Christian, and that this love follows directly from a Christology that recognizes the full humanity of Jesus.

Clement of Rome did not address heretical views about Jesus with the same passion as Ignatius. Nevertheless, both express a common conviction that faith in Jesus as the human and divine Savior is the grounds for unity among Christians and a Christian way of life. From Rome to Antioch, this was the heart of the Christian identity around the year 100.

DISCUSSION QUESTIONS

1. Ignatius believed that bishops are the only valid form of church leadership. Why? Do you think leadership structure or style matter as much as Ignatius believed that it did? Is there only one right leadership system?

2. What does Ignatius want Christians in his day to understand about the relationship between Judaism and Christianity? Are his ideas helpful for contemporary Christians?

3. Ignatius saw the docetists as one of the most important—if not the most important—threats to Christian teaching in his day. Why did he believe that the docetists were so dangerous? Are they still a threat to Christianity today? What do you see as the main threat to the faith of contemporary Christians?

CHAPTER 5

Worship and Church Order in the Year 100

The authors we discussed in the three previous chapters—Clement of Rome, Ignatius of Antioch, and the author of the *Didache*—all write about the ordering of church life. In other words, the organization and regulation of what actually happens when Christians gather together on a regular basis: who is in charge, what ceremonies occur and what do they mean, and how membership is regulated.

As in the second chapter, we will focus here on the *Didache* because this text is a "Church Order" proper; that is, it is the first among several such documents in which Christians addressed the ordering of church life. After surveying what the *Didache* says about worship and leadership in the church, we will briefly compare it with the views of Ignatius and Clement.

You will recall from chapter two that the *Didache* is a handbook for those who are already convinced the gospel is true and are ready to identity fully with the church. Consequently, there are no presentations of the Christian gospel or elaborate theological arguments. Instead, immediately after the "two ways" teaching is a discussion of baptism.

After you have reviewed all these things [i.e. the "Two Ways" teaching], baptize in the name of the Father and of the Son and of the Holy Spirit in running water. But if you have no running water, then baptize in some other water; and if you are not able to baptize in cold water, then do so in warm. But if you have neither, then pour water on the head three times in the name of the Father and Son and Holy Spirit. And before the baptism, let the one baptizing and the one who is to be baptized fast, as well as any others who are able.[1]

The *Didache* has close connections with the gospel of Matthew.[2] This is apparent not only in the Two Ways teaching, which draws on Matthew 5–7, but also in the passage quoted above. Matthew alone among the Gospels has the risen Jesus instruct the apostles to baptize in the name of the Father, Son, and Holy Spirit, and here we have the same formula in the *Didache*. The preference for cold, running water—and the amount of water used—is probably connected to the baptism of Jesus in the running waters of the Jordan. Were all early Christians baptized outside in streams and rivers? Although following Jesus' example was considered the ideal, the fact that the *Didache* allows for pouring water on the head of those being baptized suggests that indoor baptisms may have been occurring. It is worth noting, however, that the oldest internal baptistery that survives is from the mid third century, nearly a century and a half after the period we are discussing here.[3]

What we might want here, but what we do not get, is a theological discussion of the significance of baptism. This is not because Christians were not engaged in theological reflection on this rite. We know they were because Paul is already doing this in his letters and other early Christian writers would do this as well.[4] The only hints we have in the *Didache* on the significance of baptism come from the structure of the text itself. Baptism is the first step that precedes instruction on prayer and the reception of the Eucharist.[5] The author of the *Didache* is emphatic on this sequence: "But let no one eat or drink of your Eucharist except those who have been baptized into the name of the Lord, for the Lord has also spoken concerning this: 'Do not give what is holy to dogs [Matt. 7:6].'"[6] Baptism is the rite of initiation that allows one to participate fully in the life of the church.

Immediately following this paragraph on baptism, the author instructs the newly baptized how to pray. Not surprisingly, he draws on Matthew's version of the Lord's Prayer, including the command that they are not to pray like the hypocrites. Instead, they should pray the Lord's Prayer, which is reproduced in its entirety in the text, three times a day.

Not only does the author dictate the prayer that all Christians should pray daily, but he also provides the prayers that should be used each time the Eucharist is celebrated among Christians. First he gives the prayer for the cup:

> *We give thanks, our Father, for the holy vine of David, your servant, which you have made known to us through Jesus, your servant; to you be glory forever.*[7]

Then, without any discussion, he prescribes the prayer for "the broken bread."

> *We give thanks, our Father, for the life and knowledge which you have made known to us through Jesus, your servant; to you be the glory forever. Just as this broken bread was scattered upon the mountains and then was gathered together and became one, so may your church be gathered together from the ends of the earth into your kingdom; for yours is the glory and power through Jesus Christ forever.*[8]

Following his warning about only allowing the baptized to participate, the *Didache* provides a general thanksgiving to conclude the ceremony. In this lengthy prayer, Christians first give thanks for the "holy name" God has placed in their hearts and the "knowledge and faith and immortality" granted through Jesus.[9] Then they thank God for providing food and drink for all people and especially for giving Christians "spiritual food and drink, and eternal life through your servant."[10] Finally, Christians petition the Lord to protect the church, perfect it in the love of God, and gather the sanctified church from all parts of the earth into God's kingdom.

How often were Christians to celebrate the Eucharist? The *Didache* answers this question at a later point in the document and in doing so reaffirms what he sees as the significance of the rite.

> *On the Lord's own day gather together and break bread and give thanks, having first confessed your sins so that your sacrifice may be pure. But let no one who has a quarrel with a companion join you until they have been reconciled, so that your sacrifice may not be defiled. For this is the sacrifice concerning which the Lord*

said, "In every place and time offer me a pure sacrifice, for I am a
great king, says the Lord, and my name is marvelous among the
nations" [Mal. 1:11].[11]

Christians should gather to celebrate the Eucharist on a weekly
basis because they will be fulfilling the prophet Malachi's proclamation about a time when all the nations will acknowledge the Lord.
In fact, this passage in the *Didache* is the first instance in a long
history of Christians understanding that the Lord is proclaiming
the eventual arrival of the Christian church and its "sacrifice," the
Eucharist, through Malachi.

Although there is not an explicit teaching on the theological
meaning of the Eucharist in the *Didache*, it is not difficult to piece
together the author's basic theological understanding of it. First,
and not surprisingly, this is a rite that points toward Jesus, the "holy
vine of David" and the source of life, knowledge, faith, and immortality. The Eucharist is "spiritual food and drink" that is connected
to the eternal life that God grants to Christians through Jesus.

Second, the Eucharist points to the ideal of unity among Christians. The prayer over the bread, which is grain gathered from many
places into one loaf, makes this point explicitly as does the general
thanksgiving. In addition, the *Didache* is emphatic that the Eucharist should not only exclude those who have not been baptized
but also those who have divided from or are in contention with
their fellow Christians. The implication is clear: those identifying as
Christians must maintain unity with fellow Christians or they will
not be able to participate in the essential act of Christian worship.

Third, the *Didache* refers to the Eucharist as a sacrifice. It is
important to carefully consider what the author might have meant
by referring to the Eucharist in this way. In later centuries, there
were some Christians who understood the Eucharist as a sacrifice
in the sense that it embodied the physical sacrifice of Jesus on the
cross, and some Christians believe this today. That does not seem
to be what the author has in mind here. It may be as simple as the
author adopting the language from Malachi without intending it
to be taken as a literal sacrifice. It is also possible that the con-

junction between unity and the term sacrifice points to Matthew 5:23–24. In that passage, Jesus requests that his fellow Jews seek reconciliation before making a Temple sacrifice. The author of the *Didache*, who was very influenced by Matthew, transposes this to the Christian context so that the Eucharist becomes that rite about which Jesus was speaking.[12] If this reading is correct, then it seems that the *Didache* is emphasizing the importance of unity among Christians again.

For the author of the *Didache*, the Eucharist is a rite centered on Christ and encourages Christian unity. Both Clement of Rome and Ignatius of Antioch share this understanding of the Eucharist, though they express it in different ways. Clement's understanding of the Eucharist depends on his conviction that Christians should be united around their leaders, whereas Ignatius connects the Eucharist with what he sees as the right way to understand Jesus as human and divine.

Drawing on the Old Testament, as he so often did, Clement reminds the Corinthians that offerings and sacrifices were made at an appointed time, at an appointed place, and under the leadership of certain individuals among the ancient Israelites. God has not changed this pattern for the Church. There are appointed times, places, and people that are essential to the Church's offerings: "Those, therefore, who make their offerings at the appointed times are acceptable and blessed: for those who follow the instructions of the Master cannot go wrong."[13] The Corinthian Christians, fractured by a rebellion against their proper leadership, are jeopardizing this blessing. Any Christians who might gather apart from their leaders to make their offerings or "give thanks" (that is, celebrate the Eucharist) are doing so unlawfully and outside of God's will. Clement continues, "Let each of you, brothers, in his proper order give thanks to God, maintaining a good conscience, not overstepping the designated rule of his ministry, but acting with reverence."[14] There is much that Clement, if he knew the *Didache*, would have found appropriate, from its emphasis on unity to its suggestion that there was a continuation from the regulation of offerings to the ordering of Christian worship among the ancient Israelites.

Ignatius would have also found much to agree with in the *Didache*. He too believed that unity was essential and had his own perspective on the proper leadership of the church. His view of the Eucharist, however, was colored by his theological disagreement with the docetists, which comes out strongly in his letters. Ignatius is emphatic that the Eucharist only has meaning if Jesus is fully human. By rejecting the humanity of Jesus, the docetists completely invalidate the Eucharist and undermine the unity of the church. What seems to be behind Ignatius's reasoning here is Paul's notion of the church as the body of Christ. If Christ did not really have a body, then the foundation for the unity of the church is invalidated and the Eucharist, a central component to that unity, also loses its meaning. Put another way, and working backward through his reasoning, Ignatius would not deny that the bread and wine are literally the body and blood of Christ because to do that would give an opening to the docetists: if the bread and wine are only figurative then Jesus' humanity was only figurative as well. Let's see how Ignatius expresses this in his letters.

To the church in Smyrna, Ignatius emphasizes that the docetists are "contrary to the mind of God" and this has led them from the church. "They abstain from the Eucharist and prayer, because they refuse to acknowledge that the Eucharist is the flesh of our Savior Jesus Christ, which suffered for our sins and which the Father by his goodness raised up."[15] Similarly, Ignatius warns the Christians in Philadelphia against schism and encourages unity by participating in the Eucharist. "Take care, therefore, to participate in one Eucharist (for there is one flesh of our Lord Jesus Christ and one cup which leads to unity through his blood; there is one altar, just as there is one bishop, together with the presbytery and the deacons, my fellow servants), in order that whatever you do, you do in accordance with God."[16] At the conclusion to his letter to the church in Ephesus, Ignatius hopes that his audience will remain united "in one faith and one Jesus Christ, who physically was a descendant of David, who is the Son of man and Son of God, in order that you may obey the bishop and the council of presbyters with an undisturbed mind, breaking one bread, which is the medicine of immortality, the antidote we take in order not to die but to live forever in Jesus Christ."[17] In more terse and stark language, Ignatius affirms to the Christians in Rome his conviction that there is a connection between the Eucharist and the humanity of Jesus: "I want the bread of God, which is the flesh of Christ who is the seed of David; and for drink I want his blood, which is incorruptible love."[18]

Clement and Ignatius were also very clear on who should be presiding at Eucharist and over the Christian community, and this view is very different from the more fluid situation we find in the *Didache*. The author of the *Didache* does insist to the audience that they should "appoint for yourselves bishops and deacons, worthy of the Lord, men who are humble and not avaricious and true and approved," but then immediately complicates things by continuing "for they too carry out for you the ministry of the prophets and teachers. You must not, therefore, despise them, for they are your honored men, along with the prophets and teachers."[19]

Who are the prophets and teachers? When discussing ecclesiastical organization, the *Didache* spends most of its time on these two offices; the two lines quoted above is the entirety of the author's commentary on bishops and deacons. Itinerant leaders who move from congregation to congregation, prophets and teachers (the writer also calls them apostles), must first be evaluated by the congregation and, if found worthy, honored as leaders among them. It is clear that the *Didache* is anxious to prevent abuse to this policy because "not everyone who speaks in the spirit is a prophet but only if he exhibits the Lord's ways."[20] False prophets will not practice what they preach, and will want to settle down and stay longer than a day or two, demand food for themselves, and ask for money.

On the other hand, genuine prophets and teachers who can support themselves should be offered the option of settling with the community. If they are genuine, then the church should be ready to financially support them when necessary. Thus, there is a place for these itinerants, and the *Didache* imagines them as important leaders of the community. Beyond what has already been mentioned, the strongest evidence for this comes at the conclusion of the author's discussion of the Eucharist. While the author assumes that typically the one presiding over the sacrament will repeat the included prayers verbatim, just as it is assumed that Christians will pray the Lord's Prayer three times a day, this is not the case for prophets. Prophets may "give thanks however they wish" at the conclusion of the Eucharist.[21]

Worship and church order were central to what it meant to be a Christian in the year 100. Clement, Ignatius, and the *Didache* all testify to that. While they agree on the importance of church leadership and the central place of the Eucharist, they differ in particulars. Because of their concern over schism and heresy, Clement and Ignatius are far more rigid on church leadership. Not addressed to any one congregation, the *Didache* is more general in its recommendations and allows for more variety on leadership.

DISCUSSION QUESTIONS

1. The Didache *provides instructions to Christians on prayer as a spiritual practice and the rite of baptism. What does the* Didache *say about each of these topics? Did you find its advice and explanations helpful? If you were writing a simple "church order" manual for new Christians, what would you include on prayer and baptism?*

2. *At this point, we have encountered three different discussions of the meaning and importance of the Eucharist (otherwise known as the Lord's Supper or Communion) in the* Didache *and in the letters of Ignatius of Antioch and Clement of Rome. What does each of these say about the meaning and importance of the Eucharist?*

3. *We have also encountered three different discussions of church leadership. What does each document say about church leadership? Do you find one of these authors more helpful than the others?*

PART TWO

Christianity in a Hostile World (AD 100–250)

We might imagine that Christians in the Roman Empire were always being devoured by lions or killed in other ways for public entertainment. The constantly persecuted church in antiquity is an imaginative picture that authors and speakers have portrayed for Christian audiences over and over again. It is time honored, but it is also not accurate. It was possible for someone to be born into a Christian family, spend their whole life as a Christian, and die of natural causes in the Roman Empire. With two exceptions, the persecution of Christians between 100 and 300 in the Roman Empire was a regional affair.[1] Nevertheless, there were Christians who died for their faith in Christ, and in chapters eight and nine we will discuss the phenomenon of persecution and martyrdom.

Christians also faced ridicule and harassment even if they did not always face death. In the early second century, writers like Pliny and Tacitus knew of Christians and mentioned them in passing, but by the end of the second century, pagan authors were dedicating much more writing to discussing and attacking Christians. One ancient novelist, Lucian of Samosata, satirized Christians in the plot of his Passing of Peregrinus, which he wrote around 165. The main character, Peregrinus, takes up with Christians for a while, and they care for him when he is imprisoned. Lucian's readers already know that Peregrinus is a fraud, allowing the author to depict the Christians as foolish, gullible people. In Lucian's estimation, Christians reveal themselves to be fools by "denying the gods of Greece and by worshipping that crucified sophist himself and living after his laws."[2] The most prominent critic—the one who believed Christianity was a serious threat to the Roman religious order—was Celsus [SEL-sus]. He wrote a lengthy *treatise against Christianity,* On the True Doctrine, *which we will discuss in chapter six.*

Some educated Christians in the second century decided that they would respond to these attacks on Christians. Known collectively as the apologists or defenders, these writers rose to the challenge of responding to the accusations and questions raised by critics. The shortest and perhaps the earliest example of this kind of writing is The Epistle to Diognetus, *which we will discuss in chapter six. The best known of the apologists is Justin Martyr, whose defense of Christianity we will discuss in chapter seven.*

In Part Two of this book, then, we will be attending to the opposition Christians faced and the ways they responded to it. There are several questions we will be exploring. What did Roman outsiders think about Christians? What was the legal case against Christians? How did Christians respond to the rumors about and attacks on the church? How did Christians understand their persecution and reflect on it? Finally, and perhaps counterintuitively, persecution brought deep divisions within the church. Why did persecution cause Christians to argue amongst themselves so bitterly?

IMPORTANT DATES

Emperor Trajan: r. 98–117	Celsus writes *On the True Doctrine*: 178
Pliny governor of Bithynia: 112–13	Martyrdoms of Perpetua & Felicity: 203
The Epistle to Diognetus: 130?	Emperor Decius: r. 249–51
Polycarp of Smyrna martyred: 156	Cyprian bishop of Carthage: 248–58
Justin Martyr: 100–165	

CHAPTER 6

Celsus, a Critic of Christianity

In the previous chapters, we discussed the writings of early Christians that were intended for a Christian audience. By the mid second century, some Christian authors were writing for non-Christians as well. Their goal was to persuade the Roman authorities that they should not single Christians out for unfair treatment and to convince them that Christians were not unreasonable and hardly threatening. These authors who wrote to defend Christianity are usually called apologists, from the ancient Greek world *apologia*, meaning "a defense."

Around the same time, some Roman authors began to write against Christians. During the late second century, a Roman author named Celsus composed *On the True Doctrine*, the first comprehensive attack on Christianity. Later in this chapter we will discuss Celsus' book, but we will begin with the shortest, and possibly the earliest, defense of Christians: *The Epistle to Diognetus* [die-og-NEE-tus].[1] An account of this text will help us understand the kinds of questions and criticisms Christians faced and how some Christians responded.

At some point in the second century, an unknown Christian author composed a short defense of Christianity addressed to a Roman official named Diognetus. The author acknowledges the good questions Diognetus was asking about the beliefs of Christians, their rejection of both Roman paganism and Judaism, their courage in the face of martyrdom, and their conviction that Christianity was the one true religion for all of humanity, despite being such a new religion.

The letter begins with a condemnation of paganism, and the author invites Diognetus to consider why he is worshiping gods fashioned from common materials.

Again, could not these things which are now worshiped by you be made by men into utensils like the rest? Are they not all deaf and blind, without souls, without feelings, without movement? Do they not all rot, do they not all decay? These are the things you call gods; you serve them, you worship them, and in the end you become like them. This is why you hate Christians: because they do not consider these objects to be gods.[2]

The difference between the writer and Diognetus and the church and Roman society is that "Christians are not enslaved to such gods."[3]

As for why Christians do not follow Judaism, the author admits that the Jews are right to reject the religious practices of the Romans, but he also considers much of Judaism misguided nonsense. "But with regard to their qualms about meats, and superstition concerning the Sabbath, and pride in circumcision, and hypocrisy about fasting and new moons, I doubt that you need to learn from me that they are all ridiculous and not worth discussing." Christians rightly keep away and are separate from the "fussiness and pride of the Jews."[4]

With regard to both Roman paganism and Judaism, the author concludes that Christians "are right to keep their distance from the thoughtlessness and deception common to both groups."[5] If Christians are neither pagans nor Jews, then who or what are the Christians? In a lyrical and carefully crafted section, the author explains the admonition at the outset of the letter: Christianity represents "a new race of men or way of life."[6]

For Christians are not distinguished from the rest of humanity by country, language, or custom. For nowhere do they live in cities of their own, nor do they speak some unusual dialect, nor do they practice an eccentric life-style. . . . They live in their own countries, but only as aliens; they participate in everything as citizens, and endure everything as foreigners. Every foreign country is their fatherland, and every fatherland is foreign. They marry like everyone else, and have children, but they do not expose their offspring. They share their food but not their wives. They are in the flesh but they do not live according to the flesh. They live on earth, but their citizenship is in heaven. They obey the established laws; indeed in their private lives they transcend the laws. They love everyone, and by everyone they are persecuted. They are unknown but they are condemned; they are put to death, yet they are brought to life. They are poor, yet they make many rich; they are in need of everything, yet they abound in everything. They are dishonored, yet they are glorified in their dishonor; they are slandered yet they are vindicated. They are cursed, yet they bless; they are insulted, yet they offer respect. . . . In a word, what the soul is to the body, Christians are to the world. The soul is dispersed through all the members of the body, and Christians throughout the cities of the world. The soul dwells in the body, but is not of the body; likewise Christians dwell in the world, but are not of the world.[7]

The author concludes that Christians have been granted by God a position in society that is as vital to the world as the soul is to the body, and it would be wrong for them not to live out this divine appointment.[8]

Though Christians are the ones with the divine instructions, the author claims that everyone has the opportunity to know the truths of Christianity. "[T]he omnipotent Creator of all, the invisible God himself, established among men the truth and the holy, incomprehensible word from heaven and fixed it firmly in their hearts."[9] He did this, the author explains, through the work of the one by whom he created all things in the first place and eventually sent as both God and man.

The author admits that although God did not immediately send his Son to redeem the world, and for this reason seems unconcerned about the plight of the world, he was patient in allowing humans to demonstrate their inability to be righteous and holy. God revealed himself once "our unrighteousness was fulfilled."

He did not hate us, or reject us, or bear a grudge against us; instead he was patient and forbearing; in his mercy he took upon himself our sins; he himself gave up his own Son as a ransom for us, the holy one for the lawless, the guiltless for the guilty, the just

for the unjust, the incorruptible for the corruptible, the immortal
for the mortal. For what else but his righteousness could have
covered our sins?[10]

God's plan from the beginning was to reveal both the inability of humanity to reach God and the possibility of salvation through his Son. This presumably is the author's answer to the question of why God was so late in revealing himself. God was not late at all; he was following his own perfect schedule.[11]

The author concludes by inviting Diognetus to learn fully about the true God from Christians. Then he will know better how to imitate God—that is, to live a Christian way of life marked by humility and love for others.

The author of this short apology reveals indirectly the kinds of questions Christians faced from sometimes hostile outsiders: Who are Christians? What do they believe about God? Why do they reject traditional Roman religion and Judaism and believe their religion is the only true faith? As with all the apologies written in the second century, there is no evidence that this short treatise succeeded in convincing any Roman official, let alone the emperor, to abandon paganism and embrace Christianity. Opinions on Christianity were already hardening by the early second century, so by the late second century they seemed immovable. One of the best places to see the various negative opinions Roman elites had about Christians is in Celsus's *On the True Doctrine.*

First, Celsus is clearly appalled at who was joining the church. To the question, "Who are Christians?" Celsus has a caustic answer ready. Christian leaders had no problem at all with the controversial people who were attracted to Christianity; in fact, what bothered Celsus the most seems to be that they were pursuing these normally ignored or despised members of society. The leaders of the church are clearly not interested in members who are "truly virtuous and good;" instead, they go after the outcasts and troublemakers.

[T]he call to membership in the cult of Christ is this: whoever is
a sinner, whoever is unwise, whoever is childish—yea, whoever
is a wretch—his is the kingdom of God. And so they invite into

membership those who by their own account are sinners: the dis-
honest, thieves, burglars, poisoners, blasphemers of all descriptions,
grave robbers. I mean—what other cult actually invites robbers to
become members?[12]

It is utterly absurd to Celsus that God would accept a repentant sinner but not someone who has lived a righteous life from his youth.
Just as offensive, however, is the level of education and intellectual
ability of those Christians try to reach. Celsus claims that Christian
leaders are deliberately wily on this point. From his perspective,
they never dare to enter into discussion with the educated.

On the other hand, wherever one finds a crowds of adolescent
boys, or a bunch of slaves, or a company of fools, there will the
Christian teachers be also—showing off their fine new philosophy.
In private houses one can see wool workers, cobblers, laundry
workers, and the most illiterate country bumpkins, who would not
venture to voice their opinions in front of their intellectual betters.
But let them get hold of children in private houses—let them find
some gullible wives—and you will hear some preposterous state-
ments: you will hear them say, for instance, that they should not
pay attention to their fathers or teachers, but must obey them. . . .
These Christians claim that they alone know the right way to live,
and that if only the children will believe them, they will be happy
and their homes will be happy as well.[13]

The ugly classism present in Celsus' argument would not have sur-
prised any of the educated elite among Celsus' contemporaries; in
fact, they would have agreed completely. The "laundry workers"
and others of the lower classes—those without the level of education Celsus possessed—should be submissive and obedient to
those who were their superiors. It is telling to Celsus that Christians
go after those with no education because it suggests two things:
(1) their "philosophy" is weak and fraudulent and (2) they are being
deliberately subversive.

Second, Celsus is particularly offended at the Christian teaching on God. Celsus himself is a typical follower of the ancient Greek

philosopher Plato when it comes to his beliefs about God and the gods. He believes "God is that which is beautiful and happy and exists within himself in the most perfect of all conceivable states. This means that God is changeless."[14] Further, he believes that the gods of Greek and Roman mythology and intermediary spirits he calls demons exist and are the servants of this ideal philosophical god. These lesser gods deserve respect and human reverence just as the servants of an emperor deserve respect and reverence.[15]

Christians trample on both of these notions. It is outrageous to Celsus that Christians believe that God would become a human being. As we observed above, Celsus believes that God is changeless and perfect. This leads to his criticism of Christian teaching: "a god who comes down to men undergoes change—a change from good to bad; from beautiful to shameful; from happiness to misfortune; from what is perfect to what is wicked. Now what sort of a god would choose a change like that?"[16] He takes up this argument a second time, with specific reference to the human existence and suffering of Christ, the Son of God.

> To prove that God would suffer all sorts of indignities is no truer just because some Christian claims it was foretold in prophecy; for God does not suffer, and God cannot be humiliated; he does not call the wicked alone to be saved. A god would not eat the flesh of sheep [at Passover]; a god would not drink vinegar and gall; a god would not filthy himself as the Christians say their Christ did.[17]

A few lines later, he draws his argument to its conclusion:

> It is mere impiousness, therefore, to suggest that the things that were done to Jesus were done to God. Certain things are simply as a matter of logic impossible to God, namely those things which violate the consistency of his nature: God cannot do less than what it befits God to do, what is in God's nature to do. Even if the prophets had foretold such things about the Son of God, it would be necessary to say, according to the axiom I have cited, that the prophets were wrong rather than to believe that God has suffered and died.[18]

For Celsus, this is simply a matter of common sense: "Who are we to believe? A rabble of mistaken prophets or the philosophers?"[19]

Not only is the idea of the incarnation illogical and offensive to Celsus, but the geography and timing of God's intervention is absurd to him as well. He wonders why God "sent this spirit of his only to some backwater village of the Jews? Ought he not to have breathed into many bodies in the same way, the whole world over? . . . But I wonder, do you not find it a little ludicrous that the Christians take such a premise seriously: that the Son of God was sent only to the Jews."[20] The unstated accusation here is that the Son of God did not come to the important place, Rome, or to important people, like Celsus himself.

The refusal of Christians to participate in the traditional Roman religion is equally illogical to Celsus. Celsus states twice his own belief in the gods who oversee various aspects of human existence, and he was not alone in this belief. In the Roman Empire it was common to associate particular deities with particular aspects of life: childhood, marriage, child-birth, meals, family well-being, civic festivals, and other things. A very careful observer of Christians, Celsus knew that Christians refused to acknowledge the governance of the gods over any area of life. He also knew about Paul's advice on avoiding meat offered to idols (1 Cor. 8) and argues that Christians should take this to its logical conclusion: "If they persist in refusing to worship the various gods who preside over the day-to-day activities of life, then they should not be permitted to live until marriageable age, they should not be permitted to marry, to have children, not to do anything else over which a god presides."[21] Celsus is arguing that if Christians will not recognize or eat the gods' provision of food or acknowledge the care of the gods in other areas of life, then they should refuse to participate in anything the gods preside over (marriage, childbirth, etc.). And if they can't do any of that, then they should just die.

Celsus's biting and sarcastic attack against Christians must have become popular among educated Romans because a Christian writer of the third century, Origen of Alexandria, decided to write a response to his book a few generations after Celsus. Even before Origen, however, there were Christians responding to the kinds of arguments Celsus used in his book. We have already seen how the author of *The Epistle to Diognetus* responded to criticisms against Christians, anticipating some of what Celsus would write in a general way. In the next chapter, we will look at a Christian writer of the second century, an older contemporary of Celsus, who also defended the church against the various arguments elites like Celsus used against Christians.

DISCUSSION QUESTIONS

1. *In order to respond to questions and criticism of the church, the author of* The Epistle to Diognetus *describes who Christians are and what they believe. Does he provide a good summary of Christianity? What would you add or change?*

2. *What offended Celsus about Christians? Based on what you read, does it seem that Celsus understood Christianity? Is there anything that he seems to have missed or not understood? If you could respond to his criticisms, what would you say?*

3. *How current are Celsus's arguments against Christianity? What arguments do critics seem to use most often against Christians today? Do Christians do a good job responding to them?*

CHAPTER 7

Justin Martyr, a Defender of Christianity

In a brief autobiography, Justin Martyr (100–165) described himself as a philosopher seeking the truth who became convinced that Christianity was the true philosophy.[1] Part of the church in the city of Rome, Justin wrote two apologies for Christianity: the first is a general defense of Christianity addressed to Emperor Antoninus Pius (r. 138–61) and the second is a much shorter address to the people of Rome composed sometime after the first apology. In this chapter, we will see how Justin defends Christianity by focusing on his first apology.

Justin's purpose, as he says at the beginning of the *First Apology*, is to defend Christians "who are unjustly hated and grossly abused" by insisting that reason and not prejudice should guide all decisions on the guilt or innocence of people.[2] He does four things in this text to accomplish this objective: he responds to the slanders and accusations Christians face, he discusses Greco-Roman paganism to point out how the Romans believe things that they find laughable in Christianity, he discusses the ancient Israelite prophecies (the Old Testament) that verify Christians' claims about Jesus and the church, and he concludes by describing Christian worship.

At the outset of his apology, Justin addresses the emperor directly, insisting that Christians be treated like all other residents of the Roman Empire under Roman law. "[W]e ask that the charges against us be investigated, and that, if they are substantiated let us be punished as is fitting. But if nobody can prove anything against us, true reason forbids you, because of an evil rumor, to wrong innocent people, and indeed rather to wrong yourselves who think fit to instigate action, not by judgment, but by passion."[3] Though he does not state them, what Justin seems to have in mind are the rumors that Christians were cannibals or that they were involved in incestuous immorality. The issue that particularly offends him, which he raises several times, is the policy of relying simply on the name "Christian" as all the evidence required to find guilt. "For we are accused of being Christians, and to hate what is favorable is unjust. Again, if one of the accused deny the name, saying that he is not a Christian, you acquit him, as having no proof that he is an evildoer; but if anyone acknowledges that he is one, you punish him on account of this acknowledgement."[4] In short, "you do not investigate the charges made against us."[5]

The three specific accusations that Justin addresses are that Christians are atheists, immoral, and disloyal. He freely admits that Christians are atheists, if atheism means refusing to honor the Roman gods. These gods, Justin claims, are not deities at all and are in reality "wicked and impious demons."[6] It is true that Christians do not "honor with many sacrifices and garlands of flowers the objects that people have formed and set up in temples and named gods," but this is because Christians worship the one true God the Father, his Son, and the Holy Spirit.[7] The true God has no need of material offerings (i.e. animal sacrifices); he desires only virtues and good deeds from his creation.

Justin acknowledges that there might be some confusion on the loyalty of Christians to the Roman state. After all, Christians speak of anticipating a kingdom. However, this kingdom is not part of the earthly order; it is an eternal, heavenly kingdom. Consequently, Justin makes a bold claim about the relationship between Christians and the Roman authorities: "more than all other people we are your helpers and allies in the cause of peace."[8] Christians are virtuous because they believe God is always aware of their actions; there is no hiding from him. Justin asserts that if all people became Christians, then the empire would be far more peaceful with few—if any—people to punish for crimes.[9] The emperors would also have less trouble collecting taxes since Jesus himself commanded his followers to pay their taxes to the proper authorities.[10]

Aware that Christians are accused of sexual misconduct, murder, and hatred for humanity, Justin provides a collection of Jesus's sayings from the synoptic Gospels to support the rigorous morality that Christians follow. Christians are chaste, going so far as to avoid marriage altogether or second marriages if their spouses die; Christians are free and generous with their possessions toward the poor; and Christians love their neighbors rather than hating them.[11] Justin warns that only those deceived by demons would be so blind to the morality of Christians as required of them by their Lord Jesus.

Satisfied with his answers to these charges, Justin turns to his second goal: establishing the superiority of Christianity over Greco-Roman mythology and religion. Justin reaffirms the Christian understanding of God in this section as a standard against which he can measure the dominant religious beliefs of the Roman world. At this point in the *First Apology*, he has already stated that Christians are devoted to Christ—the Son of God and a part of the triune God revealed in the Bible. Jesus "is the son of the true God himself, and holding Him in the second place, and the prophetic Spirit in the third rank."[12] As he begins his refutation of Roman paganism, he clarifies further how Christians understand the Son of God: "Jesus Christ alone was really begotten as Son by God, being his Word and first-begotten and power, and becoming man by his will he taught us these things for the conversion and restoration of the human race."[13] Following the gospel of John, Justin attaches great importance to the truth that Jesus is the Word (the Logos) of God. It is important to remember that "logos" means not only "word" but also "reason," and Justin the Christian philosopher uses this word to present Christianity as a reasonable religion in contrast to Roman paganism.

First, he argues that pagans have no grounds to stand on if they wish to accuse the Christians of holding outlandish or strange beliefs. Christians believe that Jesus, the Son of God, suffered, was crucified, and then was resurrected and ascended to heaven. The Romans have their myths of divinities, sons of Zeus, who suffered death and came back to life to ascend to the stars. Justin reminds his audience that even the emperors are recognized as gods after their deaths and are believed to ascend to the stars. Justin continues with the similarities: "If we say that he was born of a virgin, let this be to you in common with Perseus. And when we say that he healed the lame, the paralytic, and those born blind, and raised the dead, we appear to say things similar to those said to have been done by Asclepius."[14] We should not miss the bold move Justin is making here: in order to defend Christianity, he is equating it with—or normalizing it to—existing pagan mythology. Why should the Romans criticize Christianity as being outlandish if the main beliefs of Christians are also represented in pagan myths?

Second, not only is it a religion that the Romans should not view as totally alien, but it is a religion they should view as superior to their own. Rather than believing in deities that are represented as animals or objects of the natural world, Christians acknowledge the one true God.[15] The Roman gods did vicious and immoral things—particularly Zeus's many sexual escapades with humans—or were dependent on the help of monsters or mortals to achieve their goals. Christians, on the other hand, acknowledge the one true God and his son Jesus Christ who never did anything similar or needed any creature to assist them.[16] In other ways, it is evident that Christianity promotes a better morality than Roman religion. Pagans desert their unwanted infants, who either die and make their parents murderers or are picked up by a passer-by and raised to become prostitutes in a temple. Christians, on the other hand, are commanded to care for all their children as an act of piety and justice.[17] In fact, much of Roman religious culture is the result of the influence of demons, where Christianity is the religion of the one true God whom the demons oppose.[18]

His next move is to establish the antiquity of Christian belief by demonstrating that the prophets of ancient Israel had already foretold the elements of the gospel.

In these books, then, of the prophets we have found it predicted that Jesus our Christ would come, born of a virgin, growing up to manhood, and healing every disease and every sickness and raising the dead, and hated and unrecognized and crucified, and dying and rising again and ascending to heaven, and both being and being called Son of God. We find it predicted that certain people should be sent by Him into every nation to proclaim these things, and that rather among the Gentiles people should believe on Him. And he was predicted before he appeared, first five thousand years before, and again three thousand, and then two thousand, and again one thousand, and yet again eight hundred; for in the succession of the generations other prophets again and again arose.[19]

Justin systematically goes through these points, presenting for each one passages of Scripture from the Old Testament as evidence for his claim that Christ and the church were foretold long ago and these prophecies have now come to pass.

In this section of his *Apology* he also returns to his discussion about the superiority of Christianity over Roman paganism. Having now established the antiquity of Christian belief, he believes he can close the loop on this argument. First, he addresses those who wish to criticize Christians for their belief that God sent the Savior so late in human history. What about everyone who lived before Christ was born? Justin's answer depends on John's identification of Jesus as the Logos of God—usually translated as the "Word of God" in chapter one of his gospel—but recall that "logos" can also mean "reason." Just as the prophets understood that Christ would be born as the Savior, so too have there been people who lived according to the Logos.

We have been taught that Christ is the first-born of God, and we have suggested above that he is the Logos of whom every race of men and women were partakers. And they who lived with the logos are Christians, even though they have been thought atheists: as, among the Greeks, Socrates and Heraclitus, and people like them; and among the barbarians, Abraham and Ananias [Shadrach], and Asarias [Abednego], and Misael [Meshach], and Elias [Elijah], and many others whose actions and names we now decline to recount, because we know it would be tedious. So that even they who lived before Christ, and lived without the logos, were wicked and hostile to Christ, and slew those who lived with the logos.[20]

In fact, Justin goes so far as to claim that early Greek writers who spoke true things not only received this truth through the logos but also were dependent on Moses who predated them: "it was from our teachers—we mean from the Word through the prophets—that Plato took his statement that God made the Universe by changing formless matter."[21] He then goes on to quote the opening lines of Genesis.[22]

Justin's argument is simple: Christianity is the oldest religion, while Roman paganism is a result of demons mimicking the truth of God's revelation. When the demons heard the prophets proclaiming the coming of Christ, "they caused many to be called sons of Zeus, thinking that they would be able to cause people to believe that the statements about Christ were marvelous tales, like the assertions of poets."[23] All of Roman religious culture, then, is a counterfeit produced by demons to lead people astray from the message of the one true God that his prophets have proclaimed since the beginning of humanity.

Justin concludes his apology with a vivid description of Christian worship, centering on baptism and the Eucharist. His goal here is to lay to rest the vicious rumors that circulated about secret Christian gatherings characterized by cannibalism and incest.

Baptism is the initiation rite for those who have accepted the gospel and repented of their sins, and who wish to live as Christians. Once the body of Christians has prayed and fasted with the one who wishes to join the church, "[t]hen they are brought by us where there is water, and are born again in the same manner of rebirth by which we ourselves were born again, for they then receive washing in the name of God the Father and Master of all, and of our Savior, Jesus Christ, and of the Holy Spirit."[24] In Justin's eyes, the key to understanding baptism is the passage from John 3 where Jesus tells Nicodemus he must be born again. This is further clarified through the prophet Isaiah, who reveals that God commands his people to wash and put away evil from themselves so he can make them clean. Just as the seed of a married couple produces a child, so the waters of baptism produce a rebirth.[25]

Justin gives an account of the Eucharist twice: once after discussing baptism to signify how the newly baptized are incorporated into the church, and again while discussing what Christians do at their weekly gatherings on Sunday. He explains that only those who have been reborn receive the bread and the wine.

> *For we do not receive these things as common bread nor common drink; but in like manner as Jesus Christ our Savior having been incarnate by God's logos took both flesh and blood for our salvation, so also we have been taught that the food eucharistized through the word of prayer that is from Him, from which our blood and flesh are nourished by transformation, is the flesh and blood of that Jesus who became incarnate.*[26]

Unlike Ignatius, who also connected the incarnation with the Eucharist, Justin is not here countering docetists. His understanding of the Eucharist—as a reality founded on the incarnation of Jesus—is simply a faithful reading of the Gospels. Jesus had identified the bread as his body and the wine as his blood, and the apostles had passed this along to future generations of Christians.

What is remarkable about Justin and the other apologists of the second and third centuries is the continuity among them.[27] The way Justin defended Christianity by appealing to Roman law, arguing that Christianity was an ancient religion, using John 1 and its logos language to explain that Christianity was a reasonable religion, and arguing that Christians were the most ethical people of the empire is the way other apologists defended Christianity as well. Despite the efforts of Justin and other apologists, the Roman authorities were not convinced and persecution was a reality for some Christians living in the Roman Mediterranean, as we will see in the next few chapters.

DISCUSSION QUESTIONS

1. Based on what Justin wrote in his First Apology, *what accusations did Christians face in the Roman Empire and how does Justin respond to them?*

2. Two arguments Justin uses to defend Christianity might seem strange to us: Christianity is no different from paganism (for example, both have virgin birth stories) and all those who followed the Logos, followed reason, before Christ came to Earth were Christians. Why do you think Justin defended Christianity in this way? What problems might there be with this kind of defense?

3. What does Justin say about baptism and the Lord's Supper, and why did Justin conclude his apology with this section? How does what he says differ from the Didache, Ignatius of Antioch, *and Clement of Rome [See chapter five if you need to review]?*

CHAPTER 8

The Persecution of Christians

At some point between 154 and 156, Polycarp, the aged bishop of Smyrna with whom Ignatius of Antioch had corresponded, was martyred. An account of his last days and death was sent from the church in Smyrna to the church in Philomelium, an inland city in what is today central Turkey. This account is one of the earliest narratives on the suffering and death of a Christian outside of the New Testament, and it anticipates many such narratives—or martyrologies—to come in the subsequent centuries.

In the next three chapters we will be discussing the persecution of Christians in the Roman Empire. In this chapter, we will use *The Martyrdom of Polycarp* as a reference point to discuss the persecution of Christians more generally in the period 100 to 300. In chapter nine we will discuss how Christians understood and commemorated martyrdom by drawing on *The Martyrdom of Perpetua and Felicity*, one of the most popular early Christian martyr accounts. Finally, in chapter ten we will discuss how persecution was both a unifying and divisive force in the early church.

Before we discuss Polycarp's martyrdom, we need to begin with the legal issues surrounding the persecution of Christians. Our look at Justin in the previous chapter has already alerted us to the unusual legal challenges—not to mention the religious challenges—Christians faced in the Roman Empire. Simply identifying with being a Christian was enough to produce a guilty verdict, and Justin and other apologists often pointed out that this violated long-standing Roman legal practice.

The Roman policy on Christians was established in the early second century through the correspondence of Pliny, the Roman governor of Bithynia, and Emperor Trajan about what to do with Christians. We have already discussed his acute observations about the identity of Christians as followers of Jesus with a moral code; here we want to focus on how he approached the status of Christians legally. It is interesting to note that he specifically asks Trajan about the very point apologists disputed: is it "the name Christian, itself untainted with crimes, or the crimes which cling to the name which should be punished."[1] In another part of his letter to Trajan, Pliny explained his proceedings:

> In the meantime, this is the procedure I have followed, in the cases of those brought before me as Christians. I asked them whether they were Christians. If they admitted it, I asked them a second and a third time, threatening them with execution. Those who remained obdurate I ordered to be executed, for I was in no doubt, whatever it was which they were confessing, that their obstinacy and their inflexible stubbornness should at any rate be punished. Others similarly lunatic were Roman citizens, so I registered them as due to be sent back to Rome.

> Later in the course of the hearings, as usually happens, the charge rippled outwards, and more examples appeared. An anonymous document was published containing the names of many. Those who denied that they were or had been Christians and called upon the gods after me, and with incense and wine made obeisance to your statue, which I had ordered to be brought in together with images of the gods for this very purpose, and who moreover cursed Christ (those who are truly Christian cannot, it is said, be forced to do any of these things), I ordered to be acquitted. Others who were named by an informer stated that they were Christians and then denied it. They said that in fact they had been, but had abandoned their allegiance, some three years previously, some more years earlier, and one or two as many as twenty years before. All these as well worshipped your statue and images of the gods, and blasphemed Christ.[2]

Pliny knows there have been trials of Christians in the past—perhaps referring to the trials of Christians under Emperor Domitian—but apparently has found no guidance on the legal procedure with respect to Christians.

His *ad hoc* system for dealing with Christians is based, in part, on Roman judicial proceedings.[3] There were several rounds of interrogation, attention to Roman citizenship, and, as Pliny expresses, concern about anonymous accusations. Pliny was definitely relying on his own judgment when dealing with Christians, and all of this was complicated in his mind because it was obvious to him that Christians were not committing crimes other than their refusal to participate in traditional Roman religion. The religious test he employed seems to be the solution he developed.

Quite unintentionally, Pliny had created the official policy of the emperors toward Christianity that would be in place for generations. Trajan affirmed this for the first time in his response to Pliny's letter:

> *You have followed the appropriate procedure, my Secundus [Pliny], in examining the cases of those brought before you as Christians, for no general rule can be laid down which would establish a definite routine. Christians are not to be sought out. If brought before you and found guilty, they must be punished, but in such a way that a person who denies that he is a Christian and demonstrates this by his action, that is, by worshipping our gods, may obtain pardon for repentance, even if his previous record is suspect. Documents published anonymously must play no role in any accusation, for they give the worst example, and are foreign to our age.[4]*

There are several things we should notice about this. First, Trajan recognizes that this is uncharted waters for Roman jurisprudence and as a result counsels flexibility rather than an established rule. Second, as far as Trajan was concerned, it was not "open season" on the church: there was to be no empire wide move against all Christians. Effectively, Trajan is telling Pliny—probably to the governor's relief—that it is not his responsibility to locate and prosecute all Christians in his province. Third, if Christians are brought to the attention of the legal authorities in the province, then the authorities must act on this and punish them. However, there are two important caveats: (1) anyone who denies being a Christian by honoring the gods of Rome was to be released immediately and

(2) anonymous prosecutions were unacceptable in any Roman court and that prohibition extended to cases involving Christians. Trajan's reply was reaffirmed as Roman legal practice a decade later during the reign of Hadrian (117–38). A provincial governor asked Hadrian for greater license in hunting down Christians, and Hadrian denied the request, citing the rules that Trajan had laid down. This policy of legal restraint, though in the context of general suspicion about Christians, was the official policy of the empire during the second century. Having said that, it is fascinating to observe in the accounts of martyrs the haphazard way Roman officials followed this policy. *The Martyrdom of Polycarp* provides one example of a Roman bureaucrat struggling with a case involving Christians while also allowing us to see how Christians themselves reflected on the meaning of martyrdom.

After introductory matters, the narrator of *The Martyrdom of Polycarp* has us join a persecution already underway. There is no indication of how it started or why; instead, there is an inspirational discussion of the virtues of the martyrs and praise for martyrdom "conformable to the gospel."[5] For example, Germanicus encouraged many through his endurance, despite his being a young man. The only hints we have on the legal proceedings during the persecution is in another reference to a named individual who did not live up to the heroic ideals of the Christian martyr. Quintus, another young man,

> took fright when he saw the wild beasts. In fact, he was the one who had forced himself and some others to come forward voluntarily. The proconsul [governor] by much entreaty persuaded him to take the oath and to offer the sacrifice. For this reason, therefore, brethren, we do not praise those who come forward of their own accord, since the gospel does not teach us to do this.[6]

The final sentence is our evidence that the provincial governor, the proconsul, was using the religious test Pliny developed to separate those who would be condemned and those who would be released. It would also seem, from this short passage, that some Christians, eager for martyrdom, were presenting themselves before the governor to condemn themselves. This too would be in keeping with Trajan's rule on persecution. If Christians were not to be sought out and anonymous accusations were not to be accepted, then this was the sole recourse for Christians who were desperate to prove themselves through martyrdom. Note that the narrator does not approve of this, and the failure of Quintus' nerve is all the evidence the writer needs for why this is a bad idea. For the narrator, an important element of a martyrdom "conformable to the gospel" is quietly waiting to be taken rather than goading the Roman authorities to act.

After naming a good and bad example of martyrdom, the narrator turns to Polycarp. In light of the legal framework established through Trajan and Hadrian, the first few paragraphs of this account raise many questions. The first thing we learn is that Polycarp is on the run. According to the narrator, at first the aged bishop simply wanted to stay in Smyrna, but his congregation convinced him to flee to the countryside. Prior to his capture, he followed their advice and shifted locations twice. But why was Polycarp being sought out? A formal accusation is what ought to have begun Polycarp's ordeal, but the narrator gives no account of this. The absence does not mean that it did not happen, but, whether it happened or not, the narrator chose to link the cause of Polycarp's arrest and martyrdom with the whim of the residents of the city.

At the death of Germanicus, the mob cheering on the spectacle shouted, "Away with the atheists! Make a search for Polycarp!"[7] Those charged with finding Polycarp then began their manhunt, moving from location to location, torturing slaves at each place they searched in order to get information that might lead to the capture of the bishop. Upon finding him, they brought him back to the city but not, as one would expect, to the governor's tribunal. Instead, he was brought straight to the arena where the mob was in a frenzy.

The picture we have in these paragraphs is not the calm, deliberative plan of action that Pliny described in his letter and both Trajan and Hadrian decreed. Instead, it would appear that the mob is in control of the situation and that Christians were being hunted and captured ahead of formal proceedings. Once Polycarp is in the city and in the arena, the governor intervenes. Brought before him, Polycarp is questioned and then invited to honor the gods of Rome. *The Martyrdom of Polycarp* contains a dramatic rendition of the system that Pliny created and Trajan affirmed:

> *The proconsul asked him if he were Polycarp. And when he confessed that he was, he tried to persuade him to deny the faith, saying, "Have respect for your age"—and other things that customarily follow this, such as, "Swear by the fortune of Caesar; change your mind; say, 'Away with the atheists!' "*

> *But Polycarp looked with earnest face at the whole crowd of law-less heathen in the arena, and motioned to them with his hand. Then, groaning and looking up to heaven, he said, "Away with the atheists!"*

> *But the proconsul was insistent and said: "Take the oath, and I shall release you. Curse Christ."*

> *Polycarp said: "Eighty-six years I have served him, and he never did me wrong. How can I blaspheme my King who saved me?"*

> *And upon his persisting still and saying, "Swear by the fortune of Caesar," he answered, "If you vainly suppose that I shall swear by the fortune of Caesar, as you say, and pretend that you do not know who I am, listen plainly: I am a Christian. But if you desire to learn the teaching of Christianity, appoint a day and give me a hearing."*

> *The proconsul said, "Try to persuade the people."*[8]

After Polycarp indicated that he considered solely the proconsul worthy of hearing his defense, the narrator explains that the death threats on the proconsul's life had no effect on the bishop. When the proconsul finally announces that Polycarp has confessed himself a Christian, the crowd goes crazy, demands his death, and decides that he should be killed with fire.[9]

Readers of the Gospels will recognize in this entire episode the same power dynamics that are present at the trial of Jesus. While

Pilate ostensibly was in charge, the gospel authors depict the mob as the motivating force behind the trial and death of Jesus. In fact, in both accounts, it is the mob which demands death and chooses the manner of execution: crucifixion for Jesus and fire for Polycarp. The Polycarp narrative takes this further, however, by depicting a death scene in which the Roman authorities are conspicuously absent. It is the crowd that gathers the wood for the burning, suggesting that it is the mob and not the proconsul that holds the power. This is highlighted in Polycarp's conversation with the governor. The proconsul is a creature of the mob to the extent that, when it comes to passing judgment on Polycarp's religious beliefs, he does not defer to Roman legal tradition or to his own judgment; instead, he defers to the mob and advises Polycarp to convince them of the benefits of his religion. If this is not humiliating enough, Polycarp, the condemned Christian, is ironically the one who indicates his understanding of the proper order of things. Polycarp reminds the governor that he alone is worthy to receive an explanation for his faith because God has ordained that he hold this position of authority; on the other hand, he dismisses the crowd as not being worthy of either of their time.

The Martyrdom of Polycarp is noteworthy for the way it reveals how official Roman policy was not always followed: Christians were hunted down and the judicial proceedings were not at all in keeping with the requirements of Roman law. In fact, it is texts like this that explain why Justin Martyr would remind his audience that Christians were not being treated fairly in the Roman court system. As one of the earliest martyrdom accounts, it is also noteworthy for what it reveals about how Christians understood the theological significance of martyrdom. Those about to be martyred were the recipients of spiritual power which allowed them to experience visions and to endure their ordeal with calm. In this narrative, Polycarp knows he will die by fire because of a vision he had, and is presented throughout as calm and reasonable in contrast to the frenzy of the mob and the weak Roman governor. In the next chapter, we will look even further at what theological and spiritual significance early Christians attached to martyrdom.

DISCUSSION QUESTIONS

1. Based on the correspondence between Pliny and Trajan, what was the official policy of Rome toward the church? For what reasons did Romans persecute Christians?

2. Did Polycarp's treatment follow the policy which Emperor Trajan had affirmed? When comparing Paul's interactions with the Roman authorities (see Acts 22–26) with the events of Polycarp's martyrdom, how are their experiences similar and how are they different?

3. The author of The Martyrdom of Polycarp *wrote to bear witness that Polycarp's martyrdom was "conformable to the gospel" and a model of Christian suffering. What was the original audience of this account supposed to learn about martyrdom and Christian suffering? Is there anything from Polycarp's experience that could speak to Christians today?*

CHAPTER 9

The Martyrdom of Perpetua and Felicity

In AD 203 in Carthage, several Christians were publicly executed in the arena. Among them were two women, Vibia Perpetua, a young, upper-class Roman woman, and Felicity, a slave. Brought together by their common religious beliefs and their impending martyrdom, Perpetua, Felicity, and their companions were memorialized soon after their deaths in an account of their martyrdom. *The Martyrdom of Perpetua and Felicity* (hereafter referred to as *Perpetua and Felicity*) became one of the most popular examples of this genre in the ancient church.

Perpetua and Felicity is unusual in that it is not the work of a single author. The narrator provides a theological reflection at the beginning and end of the account, but large sections of the text are from diaries which two of the martyrs kept while in prison. One relatively short section is from a man named Saturus, while a longer section is from a diary Perpetua kept for herself while in prison. Any writing from a woman in antiquity is extremely rare, so to have part of this martyrdom account told from the voice of a female Christian makes *Perpetua and Felicity* particularly valuable. These first hand witnesses to the experience of martyrdom, as well as the narrator's comments, help us perceive how Christians thought about martyrdom and understood its theological significance.

Unlike the apologists, who wrote for outsiders, those who composed accounts of martyrs were writing for a Christian audience. Just as in the case of *The Martyrdom of Polycarp*, the narrator of *Perpetua and Felicity* makes this clear in the introduction and conclusion. For example, at the very end of the text the narrator comments that the story, along with similar accounts of martyrs, is intended to be a source "of encouragement for the Christian community" and a

contemporary example "of courage" that edifies believers alongside
accounts of the Holy Spirit's activity in ancient times.[1]

The idea that a story of martyrdom would provide encouragement to Christians in the midst of a hostile world is not surprising. We probably would have suspected that they were written for
this purpose. However, what is unusual about this account is that
the focal point of this courage is the two women and not the men.
Antiquity was a male-dominated society and in ancient literature
men's brave deeds were the ones that provided positive examples of
courage. In this martyrdom account, though, Perpetua and Felicity
are the models of courage and virtue.

Perpetua's diary opens with her already in prison and dealing
with her aggrieved father. The narrator had already given the audience important information about her: she was "a young married
woman about twenty years old, of a good family and upbringing."[2]
There is no information at all given about her husband, who was
presumably still alive because Perpetua is not identified as widow.[3]
At any rate, it is her father who comes to convince her to abandon
her faith:

*While I was still with the authorities my father out of love for me
tried to dissuade me from my resolution.*

*"Father," I said, "do you see here, for example, this vase or pitcher
or whatever it is?"*

"I see it," he said.

"Can it be named anything else than what it really is?"

"No."

"So I also cannot be called anything else than what I am, a Christian."

*Enraged by my words my father came at me as though to tear out
my eyes. He only annoyed me, but he left, overpowered by his
diabolical arguments.*[4]

This is a powerful exchange that would have resonated with the ancient audience more than it does with us. The key thing that requires an explanation is the father's violent response to his daughter. Why would he become so angry at what Perpetua said?

Among the elites in ancient Roman society, and Perpetua's family is part of that world, a woman's identity was wholly related to her patriarchal clan and her proper name, the name by which she would have been known in public, was a feminized form of the clan name. In Perpetua's case, this was Vibia Perpetua. We can imagine that her father, in his efforts to convince his daughter to abandon Christianity and make a the sacrifice to the Roman gods, had been reminding her repeatedly that she was a member of an ancient family, that Vibia was her primary, sole identity and she needed to live as a member of this family.

All of this brings home the significance of the exchange between Perpetua and her father. By using the analogy of the vase, Perpetua is utterly rejecting her father's name and her identity in his clan; she is only willing to use the name Christian. This is all the more poignant because Perpetua has clearly had, up to this point, an unusual relationship with her father. The only reason Perpetua can write at all is because her father invested in his daughter's education. While Perpetua was certainly not the only Roman woman who was literate, education was primarily for the males of the family and her father's decision stands out as remarkable.

A few paragraphs later, as her trial is underway, Perpetua records another conversation with her father.

My father, completely exhausted from his anxiety, came from the city to see me with the intention of weakening my faith.

"Daughter," he said, "have pity on my grey head. Have pity on your father if I have the honor to be called father by you, if with these hands I have brought you to the prime of your life and if I have always favored you above your brothers, do not abandon me to the reproach of men."[5]

His claim that he has favored her above her brothers—that is, spent resources on her education and her marriage that would not be available for her brothers to spend or inherit—drives home the unique relationship he has with his daughter. But the key sentence here is the last: Perpetua's father is worried primarily about his status in the city of Carthage. The Roman world was a patriarchal society, and a father who was not in control of his own family, particularly his daughters, was a shameful thing.[6]

All of this is essential to understand how these opening paragraphs could function as a source of encouragement for Christians. Perpetua resisted the powerful forces of family and tradition to maintain her identity as a young Christian woman; even more poignant, she had rejected her own father after all that he had invested in her. If Perpetua could do these almost unthinkable things, then all Christians everywhere could follow her example and remain true to their faith by resisting the requirement to acknowledge the Roman gods.

Felicity, a woman at the opposite end of society, also provides encouragement for the Christian community. While there would have been some women and men who were upper class like Perpetua, just as many, if not more, would have been from lower classes or slaves. Her presence and her story would have spoken to them.

Pregnant when arrested, the narrator reports that she was in her eighth month. No husband is mentioned, and once again the ancient audience of this text would not have found that surprising. All slaves were the property of their owners, and female slaves were the sexual property of their male owners, which means that any male in her household could have impregnated her.[7] Her companions in prison, however, are concerned that her pregnancy may prevent her from dying with them. Roman law "forbade the execution of a pregnant woman."[8]

Following the prayers of her companions, Felicity went into a difficult and painful labor. It was at this point that she spoke the most famous words from *Perpetua and Felicity*. Her short speech was no doubt intended to give the audience encouragement when combined with the description of her death.

*Because of the additional pain natural for an eighth-month de-
livery, she suffered greatly during the birth, and one of the guards
taunted her: "If you're complaining now, what will you do when
they throw you to the wild beasts? You didn't think of them when
you refused to sacrifice." She answered, "Now it is I who suffer, but
then another shall be in me to bear the pain for me, since I am
now suffering for him." And she gave birth to a girl whom one of
her sisters raised as her own daughter.*[9]

What followed seemed to bear out Felicity's claim. Both she and
Perpetua were tossed and trampled by a mad cow in the arena and
neither was aware of it happening. According to the narrator, Perpetua would not be convinced until her companions pointed out
the bruises on her body and gashes in her clothing. Further, the
narrator refers to the eventual deaths of the martyrs as their victory,
which is typical of other accounts of martyrdoms. They defeated
their enemies by resisting to the end and often confounded their
enemies by enduring pain beyond what was thought possible in the
course of their experience in the arena.

The words of Felicity and the endurance of the martyrs provided evidence for the larger point the narrator wanted to make
through *Perpetua and Felicity*. It was not just in ancient times
that the Holy Spirit was active; rather, in the contemporary world
of this story's audience the Spirit of God is powerfully present.
This is particularly clear in the introduction to the text, where
the narrator claims that during that time the promise of Joel
2:28—also referenced in Acts 2:17–18—was being fulfilled. The
author explains that the Church always benefits from the gifts
the Spirit gives.

*For this reason we deem it necessary to disseminate the written ac-
counts for the glory of God, lest anyone with a weak or despairing
faith might think that supernatural grace prevailed solely among
the ancients who were honored either by their experience or martyrdom or visions. For God always fulfills what he promises, either
as proof to non-believers or as an added grace to believers.*[10]

Several times in this introduction and again in the conclusion, the narrator makes this contrast between antiquity and the present time. It is not clear what the writer means by antiquity. Is the author thinking of the days of ancient Israel and the spiritual power God manifested through the prophets or the days of the apostles as recorded in the New Testament? With respect to the latter option, it is important to keep in mind that about 150 years separated the time of the apostles and the days of this text's writing. To put this in perspective, this is the same time frame that separates a reader of the early twenty-first century and the time of the American Civil War. It is entirely possible that the writer has both of these periods of time in mind; that is, he is distinguishing between his own time period and the biblical time period, whether the Old or New Testament.

Regardless of how we understand this, the narrator is arguing that his audience is living in a time when God's Spirit is powerfully present. His point is that there is an unbroken continuity from God's ancient people to Perpetua and Felicity and their companions, and he makes this point in several ways.

First, Perpetua and her companions have visions. Just as Polycarp had a vision that revealed to him how and when he would die (see chapter eight), so too these martyrs have visions of what will happen to them. In one vision, Perpetua sees herself and her companions making a difficult climb up a bronze ladder that brings them to a garden paradise and she understands from this that they would experience martyrdom. In another vision, she sees herself in the arena fighting against an opponent whom she defeats. A male companion, Saturus, also has a vision of their arrival in paradise where they met other martyrs and entered the throne room of heaven.

Second, the martyrs come to understand that their real opponent is not the Roman authorities but the devil himself. In her first vision, in which she had seen the companions ascending the ladder, Perpetua described their climb:

Saturus went up first. Because of his concern for us he had given himself up voluntarily after we had been arrested. He had been

our source of strength but was not with us at the time of the arrest.
When he reached the top of the ladder he turned to me and said,
"Perpetua, I'm waiting for you, but be careful not to be bitten by
the dragon." I told him that in the name of Jesus Christ the dragon
could not harm me. At this the dragon slowly lowered its head as
though afraid of me. Using its head as the first step, I began my
ascent.[11]

Attentive listeners of this text among the original audience, or attentive readers today, might recognize Perpetua's act of stepping on the
head of the dragon as a reference to Genesis 3:15. In the following
vision of her wrestling match in the arena, it's clear that the narrator
wants the audience to make this connection.

We both stepped forward and began to fight with our fists. My
opponent kept trying to grab my feet but I repeatedly kicked his
face with my heels. I felt myself being lifted up into the air and
began to strike at him as one who was no longer earth-bound.
But when I saw that we were wasting time, I put my two hands
together, linked my fingers, and put his head between them. As
he fell on his face I stepped on his head. Then the people began to
shout and my assistants started singing victory songs. I walked
up to the trainer and accepted the branch. He kissed me and said,
"Peace be with you, daughter." And I triumphantly headed toward
the Sanavivarian Gate. Then I woke up realizing that I would be
contending not with wild animals but with the devil himself.[12]

The reference to Genesis 3:15 is obvious: while the opponent was
trying to grab her ankles she was kicking him in the head, culmi-
nating in her victory by stepping on his head. By depicting Perpetua's own awareness, the narrator confirms that she would be
battling the devil.

Third, in keeping with other texts we have discussed—such as
Ignatius's letters or Polycarp's martyrdom—this text also understands that the martyrs are recapitulating or sharing in Christ's
sufferings. They are fully imitating him. Three of Perpetua's male
companions proclaim God's judgment on the Roman authorities,

and the crowd, infuriated by them, "demanded the scourging of these men in front of the line of gladiators. But the ones so punished rejoiced in that they had obtained yet another share in the Lord's sufferings."[13] Felicity stated as much in her own claim that Christ would bear her sufferings for her.

Fourth, those about to be martyred were peacemakers. Saturus's vision of paradise, described above, concluded with Perpetua and Saturus acting as mediators between arguing factions within the church in Carthage. Although the nature of the disagreement is not revealed in the text, it presumably would have been well known to the original audience. A bishop and a priest, on opposite sides of the argument, beg the two martyrs to make peace between them, and they are instructed by Perpetua and an angel to offer forgiveness to each other and end their dissension.[14]

Those who face martyrdom are recipients of great spiritual power. This seems to be the primary message of *Perpetua and Felicity*, and it proves the narrator's point about the ongoing work of the Holy Spirit, as well as encourages Christians who might be quailing in the face of persecution. Spiritual heroes were not relegated to the biblical past; Perpetua, Felicity and their companions were spiritual heroes of the present.

DISCUSSION QUESTIONS

1. How would the backgrounds of Perpetua and Felicity have been inspiring to ancient Christians who heard their stories?

2. Perpetua, Felicity, and their companions are presented as victors. Whom had they defeated and how does the narrator describe their victory? What passages from the New Testament might the narrator have had in mind when depicting Christians who were faithful to the end and victorious?

3. The narrator uses Joel 2:28 (also in Acts 2:14–21) in the introduction to argue that the Holy Spirit was powerfully active in the midst of Christians. What evidence in the account of Perpetua and Felicity's martyrdom proves that they were empowered by the Spirit? What evidence should we look for today of the Spirit's empowerment?

CHAPTER 10

Cyprian of Carthage and the Unity of the Church

In April of AD 248, Emperor Philip the Arab presided over the one thousand year anniversary of the founding of the city of Rome. The celebrations, which were raucous and lasted for days, belied the actual stability and strength of the empire during the mid-third century. During this period, there were invasions of the empire along many of its frontiers along with internal civil strife. During the fifty years between 235 and 285, there were twenty-six emperors and several failed claimants. Many of these emperors died violently by assassination, war against Rome's enemies, or in a war with a rival emperor. Although the empire did not completely collapse during this period, it is easy to imagine reasonable scenarios where this could have happened.

The mid-third century was also a tumultuous period for the church. In the century between the death of Polycarp in the 150s and the year 250, the church had grown significantly and was no longer an almost invisible faction within Roman society. Throughout the early third century, some emperors, such as Philip the Arab, were tolerant toward Christianity. Within a decade of Philip the Arab's death, however, the church was facing a significant crisis.[1] The church historian W. H. C. Frend is not exaggerating when he claims that during this decade "the Christian church practically collapsed. . . . It was almost total disaster."[2]

The historical event behind this disaster is not a mystery: Philip the Arab's successor, Decius [DEE-see-us], insisted that all people in the cities of the empire join him in sacrificing to the gods. Local officials in each city would certify that each inhabitant had made the sacrifice and provide a certificate verifying the sacrifice. Many

Christians, including many clergy, decided to obey the imperial command and sacrifice.

Frend's words might seem hyperbolic, but he is simply expressing what Christian observers at the time recorded. The bishop of Alexandria, Dionysius, informed the bishop of Antioch, Fabius, on what occurred in Egypt during the persecution. According to Dionysius, there was already open hostility and spontaneous violence against Christians occurring in some villages, but Decius's edict changed the situation from bad to worse for Christians: "Terror was universal."[3] According to Dionysius, some Christians who held public positions sacrificed immediately; others, who were known to be Christians but were slow to appear, were dragged to the tribunal.[4]

Cyprian [SIP-ree-an], the bishop of Carthage during this persecution, describes a similar scene. In his book *On the Lapsed*, he states that there where many Christians who were eager to prove their loyalty to the empire. They not only made the sacrifice to the Roman gods but encouraged others to join them.

> *They did not even wait to be arrested before going up to offer sacrifice; they did not wait to be questioned before they denied their faith. Many were defeated before the battle was joined, they collapsed without any encounter, thus even depriving themselves of the plea that they had sacrificed to the idols against their will. Without any compulsion they had hastened to the forum, they hurried themselves to their death, as if this was what they had long been waiting for, as if they were embracing the opportunity to realize the object of their desires. How many, as night fell, had to be put off till later, and how many even begged the magistrates not to postpone their doom!*[5]

What disturbed Cyprian most was that these Christians had not even been threatened with torture or imprisonment. Their sole reason for complying so quickly was to maintain their status and wealth. They could have abandoned their possessions and property and fled, as some Christians did, and thus avoided being put in a position to have to make a sacrifice or face prison, torture, and death. In fact, Cyprian defended flight because Jesus "commanded us to withdraw and flee from persecution, and to encourage us to it, he both taught and did so himself."[6] Cyprian claims that the tragedy of those who so easily abandoned their faith is that their "property held them in chains."[7]

The persecution of Decius was short lived. The bishops of large cities, such as Rome, were executed or went into hiding weeks after the edict was promulgated. However, in some parts of the empire it would be months before the bureaucratic machinery of the provinces created a system to register the sacrifices of individuals and heads of households. Decius and his son both died in battle in June of 251, and with his death the persecution came to an end. It was at this point that the real trouble for the church began.

To understand the nature of this trouble, we will focus on Cyprian of Carthage, who was quoted above, and the church's situation in North Africa. Following the death of Decius and the end of the persecution in 251, the church in Carthage had become a battleground between two opposing factions. On one side were those who wished to offer an amnesty of sorts for Christians who had made the sacrifice but now wanted to return to the church. On the other side were those who claimed that there was no re-admission possible for those who had publicly identified with Roman paganism during the persecution. In their eyes, those who sacrificed had abandoned the faith permanently. Christians in other parts of the Roman Empire were divided into these two factions as well.

In Carthage, the lenient group was under the leadership of Felicissimus and stylized themselves as "confessors": men and women who had suffered during the persecution but had not been killed. They believed that they alone held the authority of the Holy Spirit to extend forgiveness to those who had lapsed and who now wished to return. Cyprian and other clergy might recommend individuals to be restored to full communion, but the confessors should be the final judges in each case.

On the other side were supporters of Novatian, an elder (otherwise known as a *presbyter* or "priest") of the church in Rome, who defined the position that his followers around the Mediterranean would take in the aftermath of the persecution.[8] Novatian claimed that only God could grant forgiveness to those who had made the sacrifice, and it was the church's responsibility to make sure that they were truly repentant. According to Novatian and his followers, those who sacrificed could never be fully readmitted to the church and would petition for God's mercy for the rest of their lives.

This was a controversy over the definition of the church and ultimately church authority. Did a bishop have divinely granted authority or did those who had suffered have authority? Should those who had abandoned Christianity during the persecution be allowed to return? If so, what would be required of them? The problem for bishops like Cyprian was that this was not a case of heresy; that is, neither Felicissimus's nor Novatian's parties were teaching things about God or Jesus that varied from two centuries of Christian doctrine. Therefore they could not be opposed as heretics, which meant that Cyprian would have to demonstrate why their understanding of the church was flawed.

Cyprian's book *On the Unity of the Catholic Church* was his major response to the controversy.[9] The premise that he defines early in the treatise is simple: the church is what guarantees salvation for its members. Just as the flood destroyed all those outside of Noah's ark, so too would God condemn all those who were outside of the church. Similarly, Cyprian reminds his audience that in the time of Rahab only one home—her own—was safe; all those in it were protected during the fall of Jericho. Those outside were not. Thus, it is impossible for anyone to have a right relationship with God apart from the church: "you cannot have God for your Father if you have not the Church for your mother."[10] Further, anyone who is outside of the church is "an alien, a worldling, an enemy."[11] Presumably, anyone involved in the controversy would have agreed with Cyprian on these points. The question is, then: what is the church? Is the church simply all those in the Roman world with faith in Christ, or does Cyprian have something more concrete and institutional in mind? One does not have to read far into *On the Unity of the Catholic Church* to grasp that it is the latter.

According to Cyprian, being a member of the church means being a part of a congregation in which a bishop ministers. Properly consecrated and ordained bishops are the key element of his ecclesiology because bishops exercise the authority that Christ passed on to the apostles. As a result of his admission of Jesus's divinity (Matt. 16:16–18), Peter is especially singled out by Cyprian because he passed his authority to a succession of church leaders in the city of Rome. The bishop of Rome and all the other bishops in Cyprian's day make real and present the unity of the church. Just as the church is one body, so the bishops all over the Roman world, through their unity in doctrine and practice, "demonstrate that the episcopal power is one and undivided too."[12] Cyprian continues,

> The authority of the bishops forms a unity, of which each holds a part in its totality. And the Church forms a unity, however far she spreads and multiplies by the progeny of her fecundity; just as the sun's rays are many, yet the light is one, and a tree's branches are many, yet the strength deriving from its sturdy root is one. So too, though many streams flow from a single spring, though its multiplicity seems scattered abroad by the copiousness of its welling waters, yet their oneness abides by reason of their starting point. Cut off one of the sun's rays—the unity of the body permits no such division of its light; break off a branch from the tree, it can bud no more; dam off a stream from its source, it dries up below the cut. So too Our Lord's Church is radiant with light and pours her rays over the whole world; but it is one and the same light which is spread everywhere, and the unity of her body suffers no division. She spreads her branches in generous growth over all the earth, she extends her abundant streams ever further; yet one is the head-spring, one the source, one the mother who is prolific in her offspring, generation after generation: of her womb are we born, of her milk we are fed, of her Spirit our souls draw their life-breath.[13]

Just as the garment Jesus wore at the crucifixion was "unspoiled and undivided," so too does the church manifest a "holy mystery of oneness" and an "unbreakable bond of close-knit harmony" maintained by the bishops.[14]

Cyprian admits that heresy and schism have threatened this unity from the beginning of the church. In fact, he argues that the Holy Spirit foretold this break in unity through Paul's letter to the church in Corinth (1 Cor. 11:19). Although wicked and ambitious men are the immediate cause, the primary cause of factionalism in the church is the devil himself. Cyprian is clear on this point. Observing that many were rejecting paganism for Christianity, the devil "devised a fresh deceit, using the Christian name itself to mislead the unwary. He invented heresies and schisms so as to undermine the faith, to corrupt the truth, to sunder our unity."[15] In Cyprian's day, there were two manifestations of this disunity, and he argues against them in the second half of his book.

On the one hand, there were the followers of Novatian in Carthage. They claimed that they were the true church because they alone maintained its purity by refusing to readmit those who had betrayed Christ during the persecution. According to Cyprian, they were guilty of creating a pseudo-church in which neither salvation nor spiritual growth was possible.

> *Certain people, backed by their hot-headed associates, seize authority for themselves without any divine sanction, making themselves into prelates regardless of the rules of appointment, and, having no one to confer the episcopate upon them, assume the title of bishop on their own authority. In the Psalms the Holy Spirit describes these men as sitting in the chair of pestilence; they are pests and plagues to the faith, snake-tongued deceivers, skilled corruptors of the truth, spewing deadly venom from their poisonous fangs; whose speech spreads like a canker; whose preaching injects a fatal virus in the hearts and breasts of all.*[16]

Despite all their claims to be the true church that invites all to return, Cyprian states that they are now "outside the Church of Christ."[17]

On the other hand, Cyprian also warns his audience about the confessors who offer easy readmission to those who had lapsed during the persecution. In one respect, Cyprian views the confessors as simply a variation on what the first group has done. They have broken the unity of the church and, in doing this, have put themselves into a spiritual position far worse than the lapsed who are penitent. At least they recognize their sin, have renounced it, and are seeking to remain faithful by returning to the church. The confessors persist in their rebellion against the church through their arrogant assumption of power.[18]

There is a deeper problem with the confessors, however, that makes them particularly troublesome to Cyprian. As a result of offering easy readmission to the church for the lapsed, the church now has to deal with confessors who betray a libertine attitude toward sin in general. They participate in "grievous" and "unspeakable sins" without any shame and fall away from the lofty honor God had granted them.

> Let not the tongue which has confessed Christ be spiteful or mischievous; let it not be clamorous with altercations and quarrels; after its glorious confession let it not hiss with serpent's venom against the brethren and the priests of God. If nevertheless he does afterwards become guilty and odious, if he fritters away his reputation as a confessor by the evil of his ways, if he stains his life with filth and infamy, and if, in consequence, he leaves the Church to which he owes his becoming a confessor, if he breaks up its harmony and unity, and so in place of loyalty to his first faith adopts unfaithfulness, he cannot flatter himself that his confession has predestined him to the reward of glory; on the contrary, it will only increase the retribution that awaits him.[19]

In fact, Cyprian has a biblical model for what these confessors have done. Judas was one of the twelve apostles, but he not only abandoned Christ—he also became a traitor.[20]

At the end of the treatise, Cyprian urges his audience to abandon the factionalism of both parties and return to the church. The lapsed who sacrificed during the persecution are not lost forever, but neither are they to be quickly and painlessly readmitted. On evidence of true repentance demonstrated during a long probationary period, these Christians may be fully restored to fellowship in the church under the authority of a bishop.

The 150 years between Ignatius of Antioch, who had also stressed the primacy of bishops in the face of heresy and schism, and Cyprian of Carthage brought significant changes to the size and institutional development of the church. In the face of the controversy that erupted after the persecution of Decius, Cyprian's response was to develop a theological defense of the institutional structure of the church. Unlike Paul, who was primarily interested in ensuring that the gospel was preached in the face of divisions over followers of Apollos or others, Cyprian insists that the entirety of Jesus's message, including the authority structures he put in place, must be followed. By rejecting part of Jesus's teaching, those in the schism had rejected all of it.

DISCUSSION QUESTIONS

1. Why did Decius's persecution almost initiate a complete collapse of the church?

2. The responses of Christians to fellow Christians who had sacrificed to the gods to avoid suffering varied greatly. What were the differing responses? How do you think Christians should respond to those who abandon the faith and then later wish to come back to the church?

3. This controversy in North Africa forced Cyprian, the bishop of Carthage, to think carefully about the definition and boundaries of the church as well as how he would respond to the lapsed who now wished to return to the church. How did Cyprian define the church? How did he respond to those who wished to return to the church and to the factions within the church? Do you believe Cyprian made the right call on all of these questions?

PART THREE

Faith and Practice in the Third Century

By the year 200, the Christians were "out of the shadows."[1] Christians living in some regions of the Roman Empire had experienced fierce persecution, and all the major and many minor cities in the Mediterranean world had Christian communities. Both Roman elites and Roman commoners were aware of the new religion. By the year 300, Christians were so much a part of Roman society that there is evidence of them petitioning the Roman authorities to settle property disputes between themselves.[2]

In this context of growth and expansion throughout the third century, Christians continued to reflect on their faith in a number of areas. By the year 200, Christians were giving serious thought to how to make sense of the Bible as a Christian book. Melito [meh-LEE-toe] of Sardis, whom we will discuss in chapter eleven, coined the phrase "Old Testament" to express how he understood the relationship between the Hebrew Scriptures and the writings of the apostles, named the New Testament. His project was to make the Bible a Christian book, a book that was about Christ from the beginning to end. By the year 200, Christians were also attending ever more carefully to Christology—the theological understanding of Jesus as both divine and human. Christians were also reflecting more on prayer and the spiritual implications of a Christian life. One author, Origen [OR-ih-jen] of Alexandria, who we will discuss both in chapters eleven and fourteen, composed the first commentary on the Lord's Prayer in the 230s in his treatise entitled simply On Prayer.

Throughout the third century, there was a vigorous debate over the nature of true Christianity among a variety of groups who were claiming the label Christian. The majority of Christians were increasingly looking to a standard they called the "rule of faith," by which they could determine

whether a teacher's opinions were true or false. The rule of faith—a sum-
mary of Christian teaching that had been passed down from the apostles
and that was rooted in the writings in the New Testament—was the plumb
line Christian leaders used to judge whether a teacher or text measured up
to the New Testament and the apostolic tradition. As we will see in what
follows, many authors appealed to this standard in their writings.

By the late third century, the church had been living, worshiping, and
believing as followers of Jesus for two centuries. Christians had a sense of
confidence in the purpose of their mission; they had weathered the storms
of persecution and heresy and could continue to do so. There is no better
place to see this confidence than in Eusebius [you-SEE-be-us] of Caesarea's
history of the church. We will conclude this book with his take on where
the church had been and where things stood when he wrote in the 290s.

IMPORTANT DATES

Marcion of Sinope: 85–160

Melito of Sardis: died 180

Irenaeus of Lyons: 130–202

Tertullian of Carthage: 155–240

Origen of Alexandria: 184–254

Cyprian bishop of Carthage: 248–58

Emperor Decius: r. 249–51

Roman plague: 250–70

Paul of Samosata: 200–275

Eusebius of Caesarea: 260–339

CHAPTER 11

Reading the Bible with Early Christians

By AD 200, most of the books of the New Testament were well known among Christians, and they had been claiming the Old Testament—the original Hebrew Bible—as their own for over a century. Already in the apostolic fathers' writings, such as in *1 Clement* or in *The Epistle of Barnabas*, we can see Christians using material from both sections of the Bible. Further, the apologists, such as Justin Martyr, were eager to use the Old Testament to demonstrate the antiquity and truth of Christianity.

Some leaders of the church were also thinking more carefully about what principles Christians should use when interpreting the books of the Bible. This became particularly important as more and more members of the church had no prior connection to Judaism at all. Such Christians might wonder why they had to bother with Jewish writings and why so much of the New Testament was dependent on them. In this chapter, we will look at two examples of Christian teachers who articulated methods for the proper interpretation of the Bible: Melito of Sardis and Origen of Alexandria.

Melito of Sardis was a Christian leader—the bishop of the Christian church in Sardis—during the second half of the second century. He wrote an apology on behalf of Christianity addressed to Emperor Marcus Aurelius and many other books on Christian theology and worship. There is no account of him being a martyr, so he must have died of natural causes, probably around the year 190.[1] In his day, Sardis had a large, vibrant Jewish community, and it is likely that Melito himself was Jewish and an adult convert to Christianity.[2] At any rate, there is no doubt that he was passionate about helping people in the church understand that the Jewish Scriptures were profoundly Christian.

Two of Melito's writings that are important for our discussion on how early Christians read the Bible are *Extracts* and *On the Passover*. The *Extracts* is a summary of the major events and themes of the Old Testament, possibly with select quotations from it. It survives only in a brief but valuable quotation from a later Christian writer named Eusebius of Caesarea. *On the Passover* is a highly rhetorical sermon Melito delivered at Easter, which was always celebrated in conjunction with the Jewish Passover memorial among Christians in Sardis.

Melito's stated purpose for the *Extracts* was to provide "extracts from the Law and the Prophets regarding the Savior and the whole of our faith and . . . precise facts about the ancient books, particularly their order and number."[3] The *Extracts* contains the first Christian canon of the books of the Old Testament, and, in fact, he coined the phrase "Old Testament" for these books. His list of books in the Old Testament includes all the books currently present in the Protestant Old Testament (excluding the Apocrypha) except for the book of Esther. Prior to Melito, Christians would refer to the Hebrew Bible as the "Scriptures," which was a neutral phrase that either Christians or Jews might use to describe these texts. Melito gave the church a distinctively Christian way to refer to these books. His title, "Old Testament," underscored the Christian notion that the Jewish Scriptures had been eclipsed and must now be understood in light of the "New Testament." As we will see, in Melito's mind the New Testament functioned as a sort of answer key for the Old Testament.

It is unfortunate that the *Extracts* did not survive, as it would have been fascinating to see which passages from the Old Testament Melito identified as referring to Christ or Christianity. Another of his books that has survived, *On the Passover*, does give us a very good sense of the kinds of things he might have said in the *Extracts*. In fact, it is possible that *On the Passover* is an expansion, in sermon form, of what he might have said about Exodus 12 and the story of the Passover in the *Extracts*.

Melito relied heavily on typology in *On the Passover*, and he gives us the earliest Christian explanation of what a "type" is and how it works as a method of biblical interpretation. At the most practical level, Melito saw typology as the best way to accomplish his goal for the sermon: to help his audience appreciate that the "mystery of the Passover is both new and old, eternal and provisional, perishable and imperishable, mortal and immortal."[4] The bridge that connects these opposing points—what is old and new, mortal and immortal—is a Christian reading that uses typology and focuses on the slaughter of the lamb.

> *For the law is old, but the word is new. The type is provisional, but the grace is everlasting. The sheep is perishable, but the Lord, not broken as a lamb but raised up as God, is imperishable. For though led to the slaughter like a sheep, he was no sheep. Though speechless as a lamb, neither yet was he a lamb. For there was once a type, but now the reality has appeared. For instead of the lamb there was a son, and instead of the sheep a man; in the man was Christ encompassing all things.*[5]

Typology, then, is a "hermeneutical key"; it is a method of discovering the true meaning of a passage from the Bible by drawing on another biblical passage.[6] In this case, Melito had the title "Lamb of God" for Jesus from the Gospels in mind, and this is the hermeneutical key that unlocked the true meaning of Exodus 12. Perhaps the most striking example of his way of thinking is his discussion of the moment when the angel of death stood before an Israelite home on the night of the Passover. Rhetorically addressing the angel, Melito wonders what turned the angel away from the house. Was it the blood of a sheep or was it something else? Addressing the angel, Melito concludes, "It is clear that you turned away seeing the mystery of the Lord in the sheep and the life of the Lord in the slaughter of the sheep and the type of the Lord in the death of the sheep."[7] In short, "it is the blood of Christ that the angel sees," and this is why he passes over the Israelite home.[8] To put it another way, the only reason why the blood of the Passover lamb saved the Israelites is because the true Lamb of God would one day spill his own blood for the salvation of the world.

Melito was not applying this interpretation to Exodus 12 alone; he was convinced that this was the best way to understand all the books in the Old Testament. To further support his argument, he explores the basic assumption that all things start with a model or a prototype.

> *Therefore, a preliminary sketch is made of what is to be, from wax or from clay or from wood, so that what will come about, taller in height, and greater in strength, and more attractive in shape, and wealthier in workmanship, can be seen through the small and provisional sketch. When the thing comes about of which the sketch was a type, that which was to be, of which the type bore the likeness, then the type is destroyed, it has become useless, it yields up the image to what is truly real. What was once valuable becomes worthless, when what is of true value appears.*[9]

A type, then, only has meaning as it points to some future reality. Once that future reality arrives, then the type has no value or, as Melito expressed it, "becomes worthless." He continues:

> *So then, just as with the provisional examples, so it is with eternal things; as it is with things on earth, so it is with the things in heaven. For indeed the Lord's salvation and his truth were prefigured in the people [i.e. ancient Israel], and the decrees of the Gospel were proclaimed in advance by the law. Thus 'the people' was a type, like a preliminary sketch, and the law as the writing of an analogy. The Gospel is the narrative and fulfillment of the law, and the church is the repository of reality. So the type was valuable in advance of the reality, and the illustration was wonderful before its elucidation. So the people were valuable before the church arose, and the law was wonderful before the illumination of the Gospel. But when the church arose and the Gospel came to be, the type, depleted, gave up meaning to the truth: and the law, fulfilled, gave up meaning to the Gospel.*[10]

After centuries and centuries of Christian dialogue on how to interpret the Bible, Melito's argument on the relationship between the Old and New Testaments might seem obvious to a contemporary

Christian reader. But this would not necessarily have been obvious to the original audience. The way Melito applied his statement about ancient craftsmanship—not just to Exodus 12 but to all of the Old Testament—was probably new to at least some in his audience and certainly not commonly expressed by other Christian teachers.

To contextualize the boldness of what Melito was saying, we need to think about Sardis. In this city, there was a large Jewish community with a massive synagogue complex. The church was most likely smaller and lacking in the same resources. In this context, Melito proclaimed that the church had eclipsed the synagogue. Despite the outward differences between a small and poorer church whose meeting place would have reflected their assets and a large and wealthy synagogue with a splendid building, the church represented the true people of God and the reality of God's presence. The synagogue was now defunct, and only Christians could properly claim the ancient Israelite Scriptures as their own because only they understood their true meaning.

Melito's interpretive method represented one way early Christians forged a new book out of two sections: combining the ancient Hebrew Scriptures and the apostolic writings. A second way of accomplishing this is seen in *On First Principles* by Origen of Alexandria (AD 185–254), which was the first attempt at a systematic theology among Christians.

One of the guiding principles of Origen's approach to biblical interpretation is grounded in "the rule of faith": the teaching of the apostles that Christians faithfully transmitted generation by generation. This included Christian monotheism, the person and work of Christ, the activity of the Holy Spirit, the immortality of each soul who will receive eternal reward or punishment, the existence of active and personal spiritual sin, and correct interpretation of the Bible. The first three sections of *On First Principles* address theological problems and questions related to all but the final item. In the fourth section, Origen addresses biblical interpretation and argues that the apostles originally believed and taught that the Bible had both literal and spiritual meaning. The spiritual meaning of the Bible in both the Old and New Testaments is what unites it as a Christian book.

Origen started with a basic presupposition that Christians today share with him: the Bible is a divinely inspired text. What did he mean by this? Today when Christians say the Bible is "inspired" they mean different things, so it is worth clarifying what Origen meant by this phrase. For Origen, every word and every number in Scripture is exactly the word or number that God intended to be written. The Bible is fully and completely inspired by God, and thus is a fully and completely spiritual book.[11] Origen had several ways to prove this. First, the Judeo-Christian laws have garnered a universal following—people from all nations now believe them and live according to them. Second, the truthfulness of the prophets of the Old Testament has been firmly established. What they predicted about Christ has come to pass. Third, what Jesus foretold about the judgment on the Jews has also come to pass. In Origen's mind, then, there was no question about the inspiration of the Bible. He concluded that if people would not recognize this, then the fault lies with them—not with the text.[12]

According to Origen, the Holy Spirit's purpose for the Scriptures was to reveal

> the doctrine of God, that is the Father, Son and Holy Spirit, that is described by those men filled with the divine Spirit. And then, as we have said, filled with the divine Spirit, they brought forth the mysteries of the Son of God, how the Word was made flesh and for what purpose He went so far as to take the form of a servant. And then it necessarily followed that they taught the race of mortals with divine words about rational creatures, heavenly as well as earthly, the blessed and the lower, and also about the differences among souls and how those differences arose. And finally, it was necessary for us to learn from the divine words what the world is, why it was made, and why there is so much and such great evil on earth, and whether it is only on earth but also in other places.[13]

These truths are present throughout the Bible in both the Old and New Testaments, but are revealed in different forms. Like a human, the Bible has an external form—a body—and a spiritual identity—the soul or spirit. The literal account of creation, the stories of heroes and battles in the Old Testament, and the passages providing legal and moral guidance are all important and helpful to many believers. These passages are "what we have called the body of sacred Scripture—so that even by what we have called the garment of the letter itself, since it has been woven by the art of wisdom, a great many can be edified and make progress who otherwise would be unable to do so."[14]

While there is great value to the literal interpretation of Scripture, Origen believed there was an even more spiritually rich inner meaning. In fact, Origen argued that by inspiring the authors, the Holy Spirit deliberately fashioned a narrative that would encourage spiritually astute Christians to seek out this inner meaning. "But the aim of the Holy Spirit is that we should understand that there have been woven into the visible narrative truths that, if pondered and understood inwardly, bring forth a law useful to men and worthy of God."[15] Origen was convinced that the apostle Paul had first taught Christians how to read the Old Testament figuratively with an eye for allegory. First Corinthians 10:1–5 and Galatians 4:22–31 are two of the passages that he cited as examples.[16]

Recognizing the literal and spiritual meaning of every biblical passage is not something he offered as an optional way to read the Bible; it was required. In fact, he believed it would be dangerous not to do this. Heretics and Jews solely read Scripture literally in their own ways, which led them to reject the church's understanding of God and Christ.[17] In particular, some heretics created a false antithesis between the God of the Old Testament and the God of the New Testament, originating from a faulty method of biblical interpretation. Reading for both literal and spiritual meaning encourages the believer to recognize that Christ is present in the Old Testament and that the Old Testament can speak directly to his followers.

Like Melito before him, Origen's interpretive method emphasizes that the Bible is a unified and inspired text and the source of Christian doctrine. It is no accident that this understanding of the Bible was emerging at the same time that Christians of the third century were defining Christian theology more carefully. In the next two chapters, we will look at two authors who were engaged in this project.

DISCUSSION QUESTIONS

1. Melito believed typology was the best way to understand the relationship between the Old and New Testament. How did Melito use typology to interpret Exodus 12? What other events or individuals from the Old Testament have Christians historically understood as types of Christ or the church?

2. Origen believed that the Bible was an inspired text with a particular purpose. What did Origen mean by inspiration and what did he believe was the purpose of the Bible? First Corinthians 10:1–5 and Galatians 4:22–31 were two passages of Scripture that were important to Origen. Why would these passages be meaningful to him?

3. What value do you see in the methods of biblical interpretation that Melito and Origen proposed? Are there any dangers to their methods?

CHAPTER 12

Irenaeus of Lyons and True Christianity

Toward the end of his life, Irenaeus [ear-eh-NAY-us], the bishop of Lyons (177–202), composed a short treatise titled *The Proof of the Apostolic Preaching*. In the introduction, Irenaeus explains the meaning of his title. He intends to "set forth in brief the preaching of the truth" and to provide "in a few details all the members of the body of truth, and in brief a proof of the things of God."[1] His book is more of a presentation of Christian teaching than an argument in favor of it.

In the introduction he is directly addressing Macarius, who may have been Irenaeus's brother.[2] In *The Proof of the Apostolic Preaching*, the bishop wishes "it were possible for us to be always together" in order to converse on things that would relieve the pressures of daily life.[3] By providing Macarius with a basic summary of Christianity, Irenaeus is hopeful that Macarius will be able to "confound all those who hold false views, and to all who wish to hear, [he] may with all confidence expound what we have to say in its integrity and purity."[4] Drawing on the "two ways" language of the first century apostolic fathers (see Part One of this book), Irenaeus describes two paths that lead in very different directions: "The former road leads to the kingdom of heaven by uniting man with God, but the others bring down to death by severing man from God."[5] Irenaeus explains that the teaching of the apostles summarized in his book will help Macarius aid others on their faith journeys.

Irenaeus was no stranger to confronting those who expounded a false version of the Christian faith. Prior to writing this treatise, Irenaeus wrote a much longer work titled *Against the Heretics*. Taking on all the groups which were undermining the Christian faith, in that book Irenaeus refuted in detail all of their teachings by drawing on Scripture, tradition, and reason. While he does provide an account of his own understanding of Christianity in *Against the Heretics*, the purpose of the book is largely apologetic. He is writing to defend the church against those whose teachings are harming it.

The *Proof of the Apostolic Preaching* is a logical follow up volume and is much more pastoral. In it Irenaeus teaches the basics of Christianity with an occasional aside toward those same heretical groups he addresses in *Against the Heretics*. To that end, he organizes his text into two main sections: (1) narrating the Christian theological story of creation, fall, and redemption, and (2) describing how Christ is found throughout the Bible in both the Old and New Testaments.

In the last chapter, we observed that Origen used the "rule of faith" to describe the basic teachings of Christianity. Decades before Origen would use this phrase, Irenaeus began his *Proof* with the rule of faith. For Irenaeus, the rule of faith is essential because it provides "the foundation . . . of a way of life" for Christians from their earliest days.[6] As he begins his account of human redemption, Irenaeus stresses two points: the Triune God is the only true God, and this same God created and redeemed humanity. At the end of the treatise he indicates why this is essential to understand: many have fallen into heresy because they rejected the Father, the Son, or the Holy Spirit. He admonishes his audience to disbelieve the heretics' teaching that "there is any other God the Father than our Maker"; doing this creates an idol. Others "despise the coming of the Son of God and the dispensation of His incarnation, which the apostles have transmitted to us and which the prophets foretold would be the summing up of humanity." Finally, others "do not admit the gifts of the Holy Spirit"—in particular, they reject prophecy.[7]

In the opening sections of *Proof*, Irenaeus repeatedly emphasizes the Trinitarian understanding of God as an essential component of the rule of faith.

> *There is one God, the Father, uncreated, invisible, maker of all things, above whom is no other God whatever, and after whom there is no other God. And God is rational, and therefore produced creatures by his Word, and God is spirit, and so fashioned*

everything by his Spirit, as the prophet also says: 'by the word of the Lord the heavens were established, and all the power of them by his Spirit' (Psalm 33:6).[8]

The three articles of the faith, according to Irenaeus, are "God the Father, uncreated, beyond grasp, invisible, one God the maker of all"; "the word of God, the Son of God, Christ Jesus our Lord, who was shown forth by the prophets according to the design of their prophecy and according to the manner in which the Father disposed; and through him were made all things whatsoever"; and "the Holy Spirit, through whom the prophets prophesied and the patriarchs were taught about God and the just were led in the path of justice."[9] Further, this same triune God is the source of human salvation: "the baptism of our rebirth comes through these three articles, granting us rebirth unto God the Father, through His Son, by the Holy Spirit."[10] To drive his point home again, Irenaeus confirms his vision of a triune deity whose authority and glory reflects the ultimate authority and glory of the Father: "This God, then, is glorified by his Word, who is his Son forever and ever, and by the Holy Spirit, who is the Wisdom of the Father of all."[11]

While establishing a monotheistic God who is also triune, Irenaeus is underscoring that the Christian God is the creator of all that exists. "Therefore, first, one must believe that there is one God, the Father, who made and fashioned everything, and brought being out of nothing, and, while holding all things, is alone beyond grasp. But in 'all things' is included this world of ours, with man in it; so this world too was created by God."[12] Irenaeus is purposefully redundant here. He is emphasizing that when Christians say God created all things, they mean God created all spiritual realities and the physical world accessible to the senses. Some heretics rejected the idea that God would associate with or create matter, or they argued that a different god—other than the God of the New Testament—created matter. Irenaeus utterly rejects this repeatedly, both in this work and in *Against the Heresies*.[13] He drives this point home with reference to human beings. God himself—not some other deity—created human beings from matter:

But man he fashioned with his own hands, taking of the purest and finest earth, in measured wise mingling with the earth his own power; for he gave his frame the outline of his own form, that the visible appearance too should be godlike—for it was as an image of God that man was fashioned and set on earth—and that he might come to life, he breathed into his face the breath of life, so that the man became like God in inspiration as well as in frame.[14]

Created and placed in the garden, the first human pair enjoyed the company of the Word of God who "was constantly walking in it . . . prefiguring what was to come to pass in the future, how he would become man's companion and talk with him and come among mankind."[15]

This leads Irenaeus into a narration of the history of redemption: an extended summary of God's action in human history as recorded in the Old Testament. Throughout this narration, Irenaeus is keen to identify episodes that in some way foreshadow or find fulfillment in Christ and his church. In this way he is similar to Melito of Sardis and Origen of Alexandria, both of whom were eager to connect the Old Testament with Christ.[16] Following his description of the flood, Irenaeus explains that the blessing of Japheth from Genesis 9:27 ("May God make space for Japheth, and let him live in the tents of Shem") has been fulfilled through Christ opening God's covenant to all the nations.[17] Similarly, God inflicted the plagues on the Egyptians to free the Israelites from their slavery, the tenth of which would bring death to the first born of Egypt. "From this he saved the children of Israel, showing forth in a mystery the Passion of Christ, by the immolation of a spotless lamb, and by its blood, given as a guarantee of immunity to be smeared on the houses of the Hebrews; and the name of this mystery is the Pascha, source of freedom."[18] Finally, Irenaeus attaches special significance to Jesus (Joshua) the son of Nun, one of the two good spies who investigated the land of Canaan at the command of Moses.[19]

Moses chose one man out of each tribe and sent them to spy the land and the cities in it and the inhabitants of the cities. At that

*time God revealed to him the name which alone has power
to save him who believes in it, and Moses changed the name of
Osee, son of Nun, one of the envoys, and named him Jesus, and
so sent him with the power of the Name, confident that he would
receive them back, under the conduct of the Name, and so it came
to pass.*[20]

Eventually, Jesus was the one who led the people into the land, allowing them to establish a kingdom at Jerusalem and the royal line of David.

In Irenaeus's mind, the connections between these Old Testament events are even richer. Since Adam, born from the virgin earth, had brought humanity into sin and slavery, God recapitulated that first man in Christ who was also born from a virgin.[21] Through Christ—the new Adam—humanity would be restored to its original status of being "in the image and likeness of God."[22] As Irenaeus expressed it in his earlier work *Against the Heresies*, only a human could defeat the enemy who had defeated humanity.[23] Since a tree had been involved in the original fall of humanity, God used another tree to restore humanity: "And the sin that was wrought through the tree was undone by the obedience of the tree, obedience to God whereby the Son of man was nailed to the tree, destroying the knowledge of evil, and bringing in and conferring the knowledge of good; and evil is disobedience to God, as obedience to God is good."[24] In fact, all the promises to the patriarchs and to David were fulfilled in Christ. He became "the source of life unto God," and summoned "man back again into communion with God."[25]

Having established the essential elements of the rule of faith and the story of redemption in the first part of the treatise, Irenaeus demonstrates that both the Old and New Testament point to and are ultimately about Christ. His concern is especially focused on the Old Testament, which narrates appearances of Christ before his birth and foretells in detail the circumstances of his birth, life, and death.

Through Scripture, Irenaeus explains that God "revealed to us in advance our redemption."[26] Thus when Abraham was confronted with the three strangers who promised him that he would have a son, he was actually entertaining two angels and the Son of God. Jacob had a vision of him when he saw the ladder extending from earth to heaven. Moses and the Israelites also experienced the divine power of the Son of God who liberated them from the Egyptians and led them through the desert into the promised land. Irenaeus confesses that he could list many such examples, but, determining he has sufficiently made his point, he concludes with what he calls the "message of scripture": "That Christ, then, being Son of God before all the world, is with the Father, both being with the Father and being with men in a close and intimate communion, and king of all, for the Father has made all subject to Him, and Savior of those who believe in Him."[27]

By the time of Irenaeus, Christians had a well-rehearsed and extensive catalog of prophecies from Old Testament authors that found their fulfillment in Christ. In all, Irenaeus discusses fifty prophecies, and these prophecies provided a detailed account of Christ's human journey:

> *The Son of God was to be born, and by what manner of birth, and where he was to be born, and that he is the Christ, the sole eternal king. And now, how they foretold that when he came he would heal men (and he did heal them), and raise the dead (and He did raise them), and be hated and despised and undergo sufferings and be slain by crucifixion—as he was hated and despised and slain.*[28]

Twenty-one of these fifty prophecies come from Isaiah, and several of these are well known to Christians today.[29] Next in frequency are references to the Psalms of David—Irenaeus considered David a prophet—and rounding out the list are Moses (in the Pentateuch), Jeremiah, Ezekiel, Hosea, Micah, and Zachariah. All of these prophecies, fulfilled in Christ, should give Christians confidence that their "belief in Him is well-grounded" and that the message of the apostles is true. Further, they should also assure Christians that the Bible points not only to Christ but to the church as well.

Irenaeus assures his audience that the "synagogue of the past" has not borne nearly as much fruit nor had as many children as the church. After all, the Old Testament foretold the new covenant and God's agenda to bring salvation to the nations through Christ and the church by "the preaching of the truth."[30]

The Proof of the Apostolic Preaching is a valuable witness to how one Christian leader understood the fundamentals of the Christian faith around the year AD 200. Irenaeus not only summarizes the basic beliefs that all Christians must adhere to—which he identifies as the "rule of faith"—but also provides a road map for understanding the entire Christian Bible. For Irenaeus, Christianity is primarily about the work of Christ in the world. Like his contemporary Melito of Sardis, Irenaeus believes the Bible's purpose is to be the root of Christianity and the book that points to Jesus.

DISCUSSION QUESTIONS

1. Irenaeus summarizes Christian theology as a story with three main events: creation, fall, and redemption. As he discusses these three events, what is emphasized? What ideas seem particularly important to him? Did any parts of his summary (what he did or did not say) surprise you?

2. How does Irenaeus connect the Bible to the Christian story? Is there a difference between how he treats the Old Testament and the New Testament?

3. According to Winn, Irenaeus's book represents his summary of the fundamentals of the Christian faith. If you were to undertake the same project, what would you include in your summary?

CHAPTER 13

Tertullian of Carthage and True Christianity

Around the year 200—perhaps even a little before—a middle-aged legal expert named Tertullian [ter-TUL-lee-an] became a Christian. Soon after his conversion, he put his education to use by defending and explaining true Christianity as he understood it. In the process, he would have a profound influence on later Christian writers like Cyprian of Carthage (who was discussed in Part Two) and Augustine of Hippo, the influential bishop and theologian of the early fifth century. As far as we know, Tertullian was the first writer to use "Trinity" and "three persons, one essence" as ways to describe the Christian understanding of God. His defense of martyrdom as an expression of true discipleship was equally influential on future generations. Tertullian was nothing if not a decisive and brilliant rhetorical strategist. He understood how to dismantle the arguments of his opponents, and he used these formidable skills to attack those who were undermining the Christian faith.

One of his most influential writings was *Prescription against the Heretics.* The title is important because it helps us understand what Tertullian was hoping to accomplish. In Roman law, a prescription (*praescriptio*) was a formal part of the preliminary hearing before a trial that established what issues were relevant to the case at hand. Any facts or arguments the judge deemed to be outside the prescription could not factor into the proceedings of the actual trial. Tertullian's title, then, is stating his conviction that those he defines as heretics have no standing to join in a debate or discussion about the Christian faith.[1]

To understand Tertullian's argument, we need to start with the three assumptions on which he bases it. First, he assumes that the teaching of the apostles was consistent: there were no contradictions between the apostles on their beliefs and practices. Second, the teaching of the apostles has been wholly and purely transmitted generation by generation through the churches of the Roman Empire. According to Tertullian (and as we have encountered in Origen of Alexandria and Irenaeus of Lyons), this teaching is embodied in what he calls the "rule of faith," particularly as preserved in Scripture.[2] Third, the integrity of the rule of faith, or the "teaching of the apostles," is guaranteed through the historically verifiable succession of bishops from apostolic times to the present. In his *Prescription*, Tertullian singles out the church in the city of Rome for special praise because of its apostolic foundation (Peter and Paul), faithful teaching, and endurance. It is from the discipline and faith present in Rome and other faithful churches that the heretics have departed.

Heresy, therefore, is a physical separation from churches whose bishops are a part of this apostolic succession and a doctrinal deviation from the pure transmission of the apostles' teachings preserved in these churches. As if establishing a legal prescription, Tertullian argues that the heretics have no business discussing the Christian faith for two reasons. First, heretics cannot prove a succession of bishops from an apostle or apostolic figure for their church with historical evidence. Since they have no evidence for this kind of historical continuity, Tertullian concludes that they must represent a deviation from the apostolic community. Second, the teaching of heretics diverges widely from apostolic doctrine as represented in the rule of faith. The apostles had already condemned some of their teachings in the New Testament, while others are clearly novelties introduced from outside the teaching of the apostles.

About ten years later, Tertullian composed his treatise *On the Flesh of Christ*, in which he addresses one of the fundamental differences between true and false Christian beliefs: the nature of Christ's human body. His opponents are those who believe that Christ's physical body either "existed not at all or that in any case it was other than human."[3] In his treatise, Tertullian affirms that the Son of God did actually become human against Marcion [MAR-see-un], who denied that the Son of God would become human. Against

Apelles, who agreed that Christ had a body but denied that he was physically born, Tertullian confirms that Christ's humanity came in the normal human way: he was born from a human mother. Finally, in the third and longest part of the treatise, Tertullian more fully insists the complete humanity of Christ.

In general, Tertullian argues against those who teach that the human bodies and the physical world are the created work of an evil god. This evil deity, whom they often identified as the God of the Old Testament, is different from the God of the New Testament—the God of spirit and light—who sent Christ to call humanity away from their slavery to the evil deity.[4] In this scheme there is no room for the notion of the resurrection of the body and certainly no room for the concept that the Son of God would become human. Tertullian affirms that there is only one God of the Bible, and his Son, Jesus Christ, accomplished salvation for humanity by being fully divine and fully human.

Marcion, the target of the first part of his treatise, had produced his own version of the Bible. He completely removed the Old Testament and edited out anything in the New Testament that conflicted with his theology. In Tertullian's mind, Marcion had already violated the primary rule he had established in his *Prescription* by purposefully rejecting the teaching of the apostles and the rule of faith.

At his most creative, Tertullian often imagines himself in conversation with his opponents. He begins his attack on Marcion's position as if he was in a courtroom:

Clearly it is nativity that Gabriel announces. "What," says Marcion, "have I to do with the Creator's angel?" And in a virgin's womb that conception is represented. "What," says he, "have I to do with Isaiah, the Creator's prophet?" He abhors delay. He was for bringing Christ unexpectedly down from heaven. "Away," he says, "with Caesar's enrollments, always a nuisance, and with inns with no room, away with dirty rags and hard mangers; let the angel host take the responsibility when it gives honor to its own God, and that by night; the shepherds had better watch over their flocks; no need for the wise men to be fetched along from afar: for all I care, they may keep their gold; also let Herod be a better man, lest Jeremiah have something to boast of; and let not the Child be circumcised, lest he feel pain, nor brought to the temple, lest he burden his parents with the expense of an offering, nor put into the hands of Simeon, lest he make the old man sorry because he is soon to die; also let that old woman hold her tongue, lest she put the evil eye upon the boy." It is, I suppose, on these considerations, Marcion, that you have presumed to delete all those documents bearing on Christ's origins, to prevent his flesh being proved to be flesh. On whose authority? Show your credentials. If you are a prophet, foretell something; if an apostle, preach publicly; if an apostolic man, agree with the apostles; but if an ordinary Christian, believe the traditional faith. If you are none of these—I have good reason for saying it—then die. Nay, you are already dead, for you are not a Christian, seeing you do not believe that which, when believed, makes men Christians.[5]

As indicated above, Tertullian was nothing short of passionate, unrelenting, and brutal. Here he demonstrates his main problem with Marcion: he will not accept the evidence of Scripture for Christ's humanity.

Tertullian wonders why Marcion allowed the passages on the crucifixion of Jesus to remain in his abridged version of the Bible when he removed the infancy narratives. If it is a matter of preserving God from the shame of becoming human, then surely the passion narrative should have disappeared from Marcion's Bible as well. "For which is more beneath God's dignity, more a matter of shame, to be born or to die, to carry about a body or a cross, to be circumcised or to be crucified, to be fed at the breast or to be buried, to be laid in a manger or to be entombed in a sepulcher?"[6] Marcion's problem, Tertullian concludes, is that he is not willing to agree with Paul's statement in 1 Corinthians 1:27 that God used "foolish things" to accomplish his purposes. If Marcion wishes to be wise, then he needs to become a "fool in the world through believing the foolish things of God," such as the reality that God fully became a human being and fully experienced human existence.[7]

The Son of God was crucified: I am not ashamed—because it is shameful. The Son of God died: it is immediately credible—because it is silly. He was buried, and rose again: it is certain—because it is impossible. But how can these acts be true in him, if he himself was not true, if he had not truly in himself that which could be crucified, which could die, which could be buried and raised up again—this flesh, in fact, suffused with blood, scaffolded of bones, threaded through with sinews, intertwined with veins, competent to be born and to die, human unquestionably, as born of a human mother? And in Christ this flesh will be mortal precisely because Christ is man, and Son of Man. Else why is Christ called Man, and Son of Man, if he has nothing that is man's, and nothing derived from man? Unless perchance either man is something other than flesh, or man's flesh is derived from somewhere else than from man, or Mary is something other than human. . . . Thus the official record of both substances represents him as both man and God: on the one hand born, on the other not born: on the one hand fleshly, on the other spiritual: on the one hand weak, on the other exceeding strong: on the one hand dying, on the other living. That these two sets of attributes, the divine and the human, are each kept distinct from the other, is of course accounted for by the equal verity of each nature, both flesh and spirit being in full degree what they claim to be: the powers of the Spirit of God proved him God, the sufferings proved there was the flesh of man. If the powers postulate the Spirit, no less do the sufferings postulate the flesh. If the flesh along with the sufferings was fictitious, it follows that the Spirit also along with the powers was a fraud. Why make out that Christ was half a lie? He was wholly the truth.[8]

Echoing the poetic language of Ignatius of Antioch, Tertullian drives home his conviction that we must understand Christ as fully human and fully divine: born and not born, weak and strong, human and divine. For Tertullian, this is a matter of logic: either Christ is "wholly the truth" or he is not. To follow Marcion means not just rejecting the idea that Christ really suffered as a man but also any faith in his divinity.

It is not enough, however, for Christians to acknowledge that Christ was fully human without also believing that Christ experienced a fully human birth from a fully human mother. In the passage above, Tertullian hints at this. He is aware that some heretics were allowing Christ some form of humanity, but not from a human birth, let alone a virgin human birth. For Tertullian, this is simply faithfulness to the witness of Isaiah who had foretold the virgin birth (Isaiah 7:14). It is also central to God's design for human salvation and the core narrative of Scripture.[9]

Tertullian believes that Paul, who referred to Christ as the new Adam, provides the key to unlock the pre-figuring elements of the biblical narrative. The original Adam had been brought forth from the virgin earth, soil "not yet deflowered by husbandry, not yet subdued to seedtime." So Christ was also born from a virgin in order to begin the process of renewing and reclaiming humanity from the fall.[10] Tertullian also sees this type of pre-figuring in the parallel between Eve and Mary.

> *God by a contrary operation has regained possession of his own image and similitude taken captive by the devil. Into Eve, while still a virgin, had crept the word, constructive of death: into a virgin no less needed to be introduced the Word of God, constructive of life, so that which through that sex had gone astray into perdition should through the same sex be led back again into salvation. Eve had believed the serpent: Mary believed Gabriel. The sin which the former committed by believing, the latter by believing blotted out.*[11]

Tertullian insists that Eve received the lie of the devil and brought forth sin and death, while Mary received the promise of the Lord and brought forth salvation.[12]

Why was Tertullian so concerned about Christ's human and divine nature? Does it matter how Christians think about Christ's humanity? At its most simple, he was defending what he saw as the apostolic faith and true Christianity. It was clear to him and to most Christians in the Roman Empire that the Gospels described a Christ who was really and fully human. Those who rejected this, like Marcion, had abandoned Christianity. Tertullian insists that no Christian should listen to Marcion and others who use the Bible or Christian language deceptively. Further, the Bible in its entirety—not just the Gospels—affirms that the Savior of humanity would be both divine and human, miraculously born of a virgin. As evident in the last passage quoted above, this was rooted in Tertullian's understanding of human salvation. J. N. D. Kelly, a twentieth century scholar of early Christianity, sums up Tertullian's position on this very well. For Tertullian, Christ was fully divine as the Son of God.

> *He became man, however, for man's salvation, since only as a man could he accomplish his work on our behalf. So he was born from the Virgin; as Son of God he needed no earthly father, but it was necessary for him to derive his manhood from an earthly source. . . . Christ's humanity was in every respect genuine, and also complete; it included, as indispensable to man's constitution, a soul as well as a body—indeed, the assumption of a soul was necessary if man was to be saved.*[13]

By becoming human, the Son of God could reclaim the divine image lost at the fall and would also guarantee the resurrection and salvation of the full human person, body and soul. Tertullian's argument with Marcion and others was not simply a debate about ideas; it was an urgent matter of upholding the person and work of the Son of God as the heart of Christian teaching. Simply put, Tertullian was defining and defending true Christianity.

DISCUSSION QUESTIONS

1. How did Tertullian define the church against the opposition of heretics? Do you agree with his approach? How else might Christians respond to heresy among those who claim to be followers of Jesus?

2. Tertullian was particularly opposed to Marcion's views on God and Christ. What did Marcion believe about God and Christ? How did Tertullian argue against Marcion?

3. Tertullian sees his definition of Christ as fully human and fully divine to be of primary importance to the Christian faith. Is there any other point of Christian belief that you would place alongside the belief of Jesus as God and human?

CHAPTER 14

Prayer and the Spiritual Life of Early Christians

Around the year 100, the author of the *Didache* recommended that Christians pray the Lord's Prayer, as given in Matthew's gospel, three times a day and to, in general, pray according to "the gospel of the Lord."[1] Using the Lord's Prayer once or more a day seems to have been common among early Christians, but other than that the *Didache* gives no other direction for Christians' spiritual lives. By the third century, however, there were several authors providing direction to Christians on the topic of prayer. This chapter focuses on two of them: the *Apostolic Tradition* of Hippolytus [hip-POL-eh-tus] and Origen's *On Prayer*. The former represents the spiritual practices of Christians living in the city of Rome, while Origen's focuses on the thinking of Christians who lived and worked in the city of Alexandria in Egypt as he did. Both authors composed their works in the 230s.

Traditionally ascribed to Hippolytus, a leader among one group of Christians in the city of Rome, *Apostolic Tradition* represents not so much an original composition of Hippolytus as it does careful editing of pre-existing material. In fact, *Apostolic Tradition* is in the "church order" genre and contains material that is similar to what we find in the *Didache*: requirements for clergy, descriptions of baptism and the Lord's Supper, and advice on the Christian life. What is most remarkable about *Apostolic Tradition* is its popularity. Originally written in Greek, by the end of antiquity it had been translated into all the languages of early Christians. Christians took this text with them wherever they went. Clearly a text that many Christian found valuable, this suggests that the *Apostolic Tradition* is a good representation of how early Christians thought about spiritual growth and prayer.

"Every faithful man and woman, when they have risen from sleep in the morning, before they touch any work at all, should wash their hands and pray to God, and so go to their work."[2] With these words, Hippolytus begins a long section on how Christians ought to pray and how faithful attendance at church during times of instruction will benefit them. Hippolytus explains that prayer begins when the day begins and continues throughout the day:

> And indeed if you are in the house, pray at the third hour [mid-morning] and praise God. But if you are elsewhere and the occasion comes about, pray in your heart to God. For at that hour Christ was displayed nailed to the tree. For this reason also in the Old Testament, the Law prescribed that the showbread should be offered at every hour as a type of the Body and Blood of Christ; and the slaughter of the speechless lamb is this, a type of the perfect lamb. For the shepherd is Christ and also the bread which came down from heaven. Pray likewise at the time of the sixth hour [mid-day]. For as Christ was fixed on the wood of the cross that day was divided and a great darkness descended. Therefore they should pray a powerful prayer at that hour, imitating the voice of him who prayed and darkened the whole creation on account of the unbelieving Jews. And they should pray at the ninth hour [mid-afternoon] also a great prayer and give great praise, following the manner in which the soul of the righteous praises the Lord, the God of truth, who remembered his saints and sent them his Son, that is his Word, to enlighten them. For at that hour, Christ, pierced in the side, poured forth water and blood and lit up the rest of that day and brought it so to evening. Hence in beginning to sleep, he made it the beginning of another day which fulfilled the image of resurrection. Pray also before your body rests on the bed.[3]

Hippolytus does not stop there. Christians should also rise from their beds in the middle of the night to pray. By doing this, they will be joining all creation that, at midnight, is still before God in order to praise him.[4]

Although he does not recommend specific words Christians should use when they pray throughout the day and in the middle of the night, Hippolytus is very clear on the benefits of this spiritual regimen. By praying in a way that reflects the hours of Christ's suffering, the Christian will "have Christ always in mind" and be able to resist temptation.[5]

Taking advantage of opportunities for Christian instruction also enables the Christian to resist sin. Gathering at church early in the morning when such meetings occur is essential for the spiritual growth of a Christian because "it is God whom [the Christian] hears in the one who instructs."[6] Failure to attend not only robs a believer of receiving such instruction but also increases the chance of sin throughout the rest of the day. Therefore it is with some urgency that Hippolytus advises Christians to attend:

> Let none of you be late in the church, the place where teaching is given. Then it shall be given to the speaker to say things profitable to all, and you will hear things of which you would not think, and profit from things which the Holy Spirit will give you through the one who instructs. In this way your faith will be strengthened in regard to matters about which you heard. What you ought to do in your house will also be told in this place. Therefore let everyone hurry in coming to the assembly, the place where the Holy Spirit abounds.[7]

For Hippolytus, the idea that the Holy Spirit is present when the faithful gather together provides a powerful argument in favor of frequent gatherings. As a result, corporate prayer and corporate instruction is essential for the Christian life.

Origen of Alexandria, writing around the same time as Hippolytus but on the other side of the Mediterranean, completely agreed with him. He wrote his short treatise *On Prayer* as his response to some questions his married friends Ambrose and Tatiana had sent him. In the process, he produced the first extensive treatment of the spiritual discipline prayer in church history and the first commentary on the Lord's Prayer.

He begins his treatise with a discussion of prayer in general. Following Romans 8:26, he argues that understanding prayer means addressing two things that Paul himself was uncertain about: what

Christians ought to pray—the words of the prayer—and how Christians ought to pray—the state or disposition of the person praying.[8] In the case of the former, Origen points out that in the Gospels Jesus often commands his followers to pray about certain things: for those who mistreat you, to not be led into temptation, or that the Lord would send workers into his harvest. He also commands his followers to use meaningful words when praying instead of empty phrases. In the case of how Christians should pray, he draws on 1 Timothy—where Christians are encouraged to be without anger or quarreling—and on the Gospels—where Jesus commands the believer to seek reconciliation and forgiveness in order for God to attend to their prayers.[9]

Further, Origen insists that "the Spirit prays in the hearts of the saints."[10] The capacity of humans to understand what to pray and how to pray is directly related to the presence of the Spirit in a person's life. "For our mind would not even be able to pray unless the Spirit prayed for it as if obeying it, so that we cannot even sing and hymn the Father in Christ with proper rhythm, melody, measure, and harmony unless the Spirit who searches everything, even the depths of God (1 Cor. 2:10), first praises and hymns Him whose depths he has searched out."[11] Because of this active and necessary presence of the Spirit, Origen believed that prayer could powerfully change a person: "the soul becomes more spiritual," which leads to the "transformation of the entire personality."[12] Not only does the Spirit graciously assist Christians in their prayers, but Scripture also provides examples of "truly spiritual" prayers—prayers through the Spirit—that can guide and assist an individual's prayer life, such as Hannah's prayer from 1 Samuel, Hezekiah's prayer from 2 Kings, or many of the Psalms.[13]

When he turns to the Lord's Prayer, Origen urges Christians to consider it a model infused with spiritual power. One of the points he makes is that this prayer represents God doing something new with his people. Although parent/child language is used in the Old Testament to describe God's relationship with the ancient Israelites, nowhere did God invite or command his people to call him "Father" in prayer. Through the "savior," as Origen often calls

Christ in this text, God has initiated a new and closer relationship with his people.[14] Another point he makes is that Christians should understand that when asking for "daily bread," we are not so much asking for physical food as we are asking for spiritual food. As we have already seen, Origen often looked for spiritual meaning in the Bible, arguing that the literal meaning often conceals a deeper spiritual one, and here he is no different (see chapter eleven). Interpreting this petition in the Lord's Prayer, then, requires reading it with John 6 in mind. Jesus identified himself as the bread of life, and this is what Christians are requesting when asking their heavenly Father for daily bread.[15]

Origen answers several questions in this final section of the treatise. One is: what posture should Christians assume when praying? This question is not so much about the posture of the body as the posture of the soul. Christians should not come to prayer thoughtlessly or idly; instead, they should come to prayer in the right way:

> Thus it seems to me that the person who is about to come to prayer should withdraw for a little and prepare himself, and so become more attentive and active for the whole of his prayer. He should cast away all temptation and troubling thoughts and remind himself so far as he is able of the majesty whom he approaches, and that it is impious to approach Him carelessly, sluggishly, and disdainfully; and he should put away all extraneous things. This is how he should come to prayer, stretching out his soul, as it were, instead of his hands, straining his mind toward God instead of his eyes, raising his governing reason from the ground and standing it before the Lord of all instead of standing.[16]

One might think from this that Origen had no opinion at all on the physical posture Christians should use when praying, but he did have a posture in mind. In fact, the very posture he recommends is the one he invites his readers to imagine in the passage above. "Although there are a great many different positions for the body, he should not doubt that the position with the hands outstretched and the eyes lifted up is to be preferred before all others, because it bears in prayer the image of characteristics befitting the soul and applies it to the body."[17] This position, standing with arms raised and looking up, ought to be the most common posture as it reflects an attitude of worship. He does admit that not everyone might be able to stand because of disability or sickness. In those cases, sitting or even reclining is acceptable.

As much as he recommends it, Origen recognizes that this position is not appropriate for all forms of prayer. The confession of sin, he advises, requires a different posture.

> *Kneeling is necessary when someone is going to speak against his own sins before God, since his is making supplication for their healing and their forgiveness. We must understand that it symbolizes someone who has fallen down and become obedient, since Paul says, "For this reason I bow my knees before the Father, from whom every family in heaven and on earth is named" (Eph. 3:14–15).*[18]

Physical kneeling is the outward sign of an inward spiritual state of kneeling. It reflects sorrow for sin and a recognition that all ought to humble themselves before God.

Where should Christians pray? This is the second question Origen addresses and his initial answer is simple: "every place is suitable for prayer if a person prays well."[19] Nevertheless, for the devotional prayers of an individual, he suggests that a dedicated space might be useful. "But everyone may have, if I may put it this way, a holy place set aside and chosen in his own house, if possible, for accomplishing his prayers in quiet and without distraction."[20] His only warning is that it should be a place that is truly dedicated to prayer and not also used for worldly or mundane activities.

Not only should the individual Christian pray in their own place of prayer, they should also gather with other Christians to pray. Origen insists on this: "Let no one disdain prayers in the churches, since they have something exceptional for the person who assembles in them genuinely."[21] Based on his reading of Scripture, Origen, like his contemporary Hippolytus in Rome, believed God offers "gracious help" to believers when they are gathered for communal prayer:

Angelic powers are placed near the throngs of believers, as well
as the powers of our Lord and Savior Himself, and the spirits of
the saints—I think both of those who have already fallen asleep
and clearly of those who are still alive, even though it is not easy
to say how. Concerning angels we must reason this way. Suppose
the angel of the Lord encamps around those who fear him, and
delivers them (Psalm 34:7); and suppose Jacob tells the truth not
only about himself but also about all those who rely on God when
he says to the understanding person, "The angel who delivers me
from all these evils" (Gen. 48:16). It is likely, then, that when a
great number of people are assembled genuinely for the glory of
Christ, each one's angel, who is around each of those who fear him,
encamps with that man whom he is believed to guard and order.
As a result, when the saints are gathered together, there is a double
Church, one of men and the other of angels.[22]

The opposite is also true. An assembly of people who have given
themselves over to sin and wickedness will not experience attention
from angels or the presence of God. Drawing on Isaiah's criticism of
the people of Judah, Origen claims that God will not attend to their
prayers and will turn away from them.[23] This explains his discussion of the physical and spiritual posture of prayer more fully. All
of heaven—the angels and the Lord—will attend to the prayers of
those spiritually and physically straining toward God in worship or
in confession of sin. Just as a gathering of such people will bring a
manifestation of spiritual power, so too a gathering of people for reasons other than worship or confession will bring spiritual desolation.

Whether standing or kneeling, Origen also recommends that
Christians physically orient themselves to face east, "since this is a
symbolic expression of the soul's looking for the rising of the true
Light."[24] When praying indoors, it is not enough to face the source
of light, whether it is coming from a door or a window. Doors and
windows, he explains, are arbitrary. It is always preferable to face
east, even if that means praying while facing a wall.

While Hippolytus does not insist on a particular direction for
Christians in Rome to pray or mention some of the other items

Origen discusses in his treatise, it is remarkable how similar they are. Both recognize that prayer is essential to Christian growth, that gathering with other Christians for prayer is even more powerful, and that a life of prayer is intimately connected with the work of the Holy Spirit. Among Christians in Alexandria and Rome in the third century and certainly other places as well, a prayerful life was understood to be a mark of a true Christian life.

DISCUSSION QUESTIONS

1. What does Hippolytus emphasize about the importance of prayer in the life of a Christian? Which of his ideas do you find useful for Christians living in the twenty-first century?

2. Origen recommends paying attention to prayers in the Bible, such as Hannah's prayer (1 Sam. 1:9–18) and the prayer of Hezekiah (2 Kings 20:1–9). How do these prayers relate to what Origen emphasizes about the importance of prayer in the life of a Christian? Which of his ideas do you find useful for Christians living in the twenty-first century?

3. Are there other aspects of prayer neither Origen nor Hippolytus discuss that you think are important for the life of a Christian?

CHAPTER 15

Eusebius of Caesarea:
After Two Hundred Years

At some point in the 290s, Eusebius [you-SEE-be-us], the bishop of Caesarea, completed the first edition of his *Ecclesiastical History*.[1] He intended it as a retrospective description and defense of Christianity. To conclude this study of Christianity in the Roman Empire, we will draw on Eusebius for two reasons: first to view through his eyes what he saw as essential Christian characteristics after two hundred years, and second to consider two events of the third century that, in his mind, provide evidence for the unique identity of Christians in the Roman Empire.

The first section of the history, Book I, is more of a theological introduction in the spirit of the second-century apologists like Justin Martyr.[2] He addresses one of the basic complaints against Christianity: how could such a new religion claim to be the one true religion? Eusebius's answer, like the answer of his predecessors, was to argue that while the name Christian was new, the faith and way of life it represented was not. All the spiritual heroes of the Old Testament, such as Abraham and Moses, were followers of Christ— followers of the pre-incarnate Son of God—before Christianity.[3] The history of the church is only the most recent chapter in a very old story of God's involvement in human affairs; in other words, it is simply a continuation of the biblical story.[4]

In Books II through VII Eusebius begins his historical narrative of the church, and several of the themes and individuals he highlights are items we have already discussed in this book. He praises the "apostolic men"—those who were the immediate successors of the apostles—and he singles out Ignatius of Antioch and Clement of Rome among them.[5] He particularly praises them for their faithfulness to the apostle's message as recorded in the New Testament and the way they "passed on" the apostles' teaching to their own generation.[6]

He also recalls several instances of persecution, including the martyrdom of Polycarp, and praises the courage and faithfulness of the martyrs. For Eusebius, the martyrs were victors who overcame the irrational wickedness of the hostile Roman state.[7] Similarly, he highlights the apologists, such as Justin Martyr, who wrote to defend Christianity.[8] He praises other figures of the second century for their faithful witness, including Melito of Sardis and Irenaeus of Lyons.[9] Finally, he has much to say about Origen of Alexandria. In fact, almost the entirety of Book VI of his *History* is devoted to Origen, whom Eusebius describes as a biblical scholar and defender of Christianity against heresy.[10]

For Eusebius, the Church in the Roman Empire was best understood through the heroic biographies of Christians, both clergy and laity, who taught and lived true Christianity in the face of opposition from the Roman state. Two other concerns that predominate in his *History* also define how he understands Christianity as a historical faith. First, he believed it was important for his readers to know the origin of the New Testament. At the outset of Book III, Eusebius wrote, "In the course of my narrative I shall take care to indicate in each period which of the Church writers of the time used the various disputed books; their comments on the canonical and recognized Scriptures; and their remarks about the other sort."[11] Eusebius is using two technical terms here to define his criteria: "recognized" and "disputed." According to him, all churches around the Mediterranean recognize the books that are truly from the hand of an apostle, and all of these books are in the New Testament.[12] This is important, Eusebius explains, because there were other writings circulating that sounded like New Testament writings—such as the Gospel of Peter or the Gospel of Thomas or the Acts of Andrew—but originated among heretics. These writings do not at all reflect the teaching of the apostles as presented in the books recognized by the church and none of the churches have ever recognized them as coming from the hand of an apostle.

Concern for understanding the canon of the New Testament is directly linked with his interest to narrate the origin of heresy and its constant attempt to undermine the church. Eusebius traces all heresy to the figure of Simon Magus mentioned in the New Testament book of Acts. "Simon, we are given to understand, was the prime author of every heresy. From this time to our own those who follow his lead, while pretending to accept that sober Christian philosophy which through purity of life won universal fame, are as devoted to the idolatrous superstition from which they seemed to have escaped."[13] Eusebius presents Simon as the original heretic whose false teaching had been passed on generation by generation by those who wished to oppose the true teaching of the apostles. Throughout his *History*, Eusebius dutifully provided the names of the successors of the apostles in the major churches around the Mediterranean while also providing the names and ideas of the heretics who opposed them.

As Eusebius looked back from his vantage point in the 290s, he saw that his task was to narrate the latest edition of the story of God's people who were faithful and virtuous even in the face of opposition. He saw heroic Christians not only in the distant past but even in events only a generation removed from his own day. His account of how Christians responded to the plague of the 250s and to the heretical bishop Paul of Samosata in the 260s is in keeping with the story he wished to tell about Christians.

One of the figures from the previous generation whom Eusebius revered was Dionysius [die-oh-NIS-ee-us], the bishop of Alexandria (247–64). He guided the church in Alexandria through tumultuous times, and Eusebius is our main source for an account of his life. Mob violence against Christians early in his ministry soon became the state-sponsored persecution of Emperor Decius, the same persecution Cyprian of Carthage faced. Only months after the death of Decius and the end of his persecution, a terrible plague devastated Egypt and other parts of the Roman world in 252. Dionysius discusses these events in several letters to his fellow clergy in Egypt, and Eusebius quotes extensively from these letters in his section on Dionysius. In one of these letters, Dionysius situates the outbreak of plague in the context of the social unrest that gripped the Roman world following the death of Decius:

> *But when both we and they [the pagans] had been allowed a tiny breathing-space, out of the blue came this disease, a thing more terrifying to them than any terror, more frightful than any disaster whatever. . . . To us it was not that, but a schooling and testing as valuable as all our earlier trials; for it did not pass over us, though its full impact fell on the heathen.*[14]

Most historians today believe that this plague was either smallpox or measles and may represent the first instance of a human population experiencing this disease.[15]

Dionysius had a very specific reason for discussing the plague in this letter; it demonstrates the stark difference between the Christian and pagan populations of Egypt. Presumably this is why Eusebius quotes the letter at length. It provides evidence for the point he wanted to make about the church as the unique people of God, wholly different from the pagan society in which it resided. From the first appearance of the disease, Dionysius says that the pagans "pushed the sufferers away and fled from their dearest, throwing them into the roads before they were dead and treating unburied corpses as dirt, hoping thereby to avert the spread and contagion of the fatal disease; but do what they might, they found it difficult to escape."[16]

While non-Christians were attempting to flee and even abandoned family members in the process, Christians acted very differently:

> *Most of our brother-Christians showed unbounded love and loyalty, never sparing themselves and thinking only of one another. Heedless of the danger, they took charge of the sick, attending to their every need and ministering to them in Christ, and with them departed this life serenely happy; for they were infected by others with the disease, drawing on themselves the sickness of their*

neighbors and cheerfully accepting their pains. Many, in nurs-
ing and curing others, transferred their death to themselves and
died in their stead, turning the common formula that is normally
an empty courtesy into a reality: "Your humble servant bids you
good-bye." The best of our brothers lost their lives in this manner, a
number of presbyters, deacons, and laymen winning high com-
mendation, so that death in this form, the result of great piety and
strong faith, seems in every way equal to martyrdom.[17]

The care that these Christians show for their neighbors, whether believers or not, is something Dionysius wants to emphasize. Referring to the sick, Dionysius claims that Christians "carried them on their shoulders, and laid them out; they clung to them, embraced them, washed them, and wrapped them in grave clothes. Very soon, the same services were done for them, since those left behind were constantly following those gone before."[18]

Though he does not provide any commentary on Dionysius's account of the plague in this letter, Eusebius must have hoped that the stories alone would inspire his audience as much as his stories about martyrs refusing to recant under torture. Rodney Stark, a contemporary scholar of early Christianity, argues that the Christian response to plague in the late third century is an important indicator of why Christianity was so successful in attracting new converts. If Dionysius's letter is accurate, then when the plague moved through an area the recovery rate among Christians would be far higher than among pagans. In addition, pagans that did survive probably survived because of Christian care. While the church may have still been a minority of the population after the plague, it was a much larger minority and would have attracted even more converts because of the evident care the church provided.[19] In Stark's estimation, Eusebius was right to highlight the Christian response to the plague as a defining characteristic of the new religion.

Inspiring courage and faithfulness in the persecution and plague is one part of the story Eusebius tells about the third-century church. The other is its ongoing struggle to define what Christians believed about Jesus. As we have already seen, this was a question that appeared repeatedly among Christians, and Eusebius high-lights these arguments in his *History*. During the late third century, this argument centered around the figure of Paul of Samosata, the bishop of Antioch from 260–68. Eusebius devoted several pages of his *History* to an account of him, particularly focusing on the synod that judged him. Eusebius included the only contemporary document we have of this event: an account of the council sent to the bishops of Rome and Alexandria. Clergy from around the eastern Mediterranean gathered in Antioch and deposed him from his position as bishop and elected a new bishop to replace him when they found him unrepentant on the question of his beliefs and his way of life.

Eusebius highlights two reasons for their decision. First, Eusebius claims that Paul "held low, degraded opinions about Christ, in defiance of the Church's teaching, regarding him as in his nature just an ordinary man."[20] In the letter that Eusebius includes in his account of Paul, the bishops stated this same opinion about Paul's views on Christ: "He will not admit that the Son of God came down from heaven—as we shall explain more fully later, not merely stating the fact but proving it from passage after passage of the attached notes, especially where he says that Jesus Christ is 'from below.' "[21] It seems that Paul held to a form of "adoptionism," a belief that was sometimes expressed in the early church as an explanation for the mystery of the incarnation. In this view, God adopted an ordinary man, Jesus, as his son, and his baptism was often identified as the moment of adoption. The church repeatedly rejected this idea, as it was contrary to Scripture and the teachings of the apostles, and this may be why Eusebius does not detail Paul's theology at length.[22]

The second reason for the decision of the council is the one they spend far more time on and the one that Eusebius himself highlights. In a book where the author wants to argue that the Christian way of life is different than the pagans,' it is perhaps not surprising that Eusebius would find Paul worthy of condemnation and is eager to quote the council's judgment on his life in full. According to the council,

[Paul] has amassed immense wealth by committing illegalities, robbing churches, and black-mailing his fellow Christians. He deprives the injured of their rights, promising them help if they will pay for it but breaking his word to them, and makes easy money out of the readiness of those entangled in court proceedings to buy relief from their persecutors. In fact, he regards religion as a way of making money. . . . [H]e is ambitious and arrogant, decking himself out with worldly honors and anxious to be called ducenarius[23] rather than bishop, and swaggers in city squares, reading letters aloud or dictating them as he walks in public surrounded by a numerous bodyguard, some in front and some behind. The result is that the faith is regarded with distaste and hatred because of his self-importance and inflated pride. . . . All hymns to our Lord Jesus Christ he has banned as modern compositions of modern writers, but he arranges for women to sing hymns to himself in the middle of the church on the great day of the Easter Festival: one would shudder to hear them! . . . And what of his 'spiritual brides,' as the people of Antioch call them? And those of his presbyters and deacons, with whom he joins in concealing this and their other incurable sins, though he knows all about them, so as to have them under his thumb, too frightened on their own account to accuse him of his offenses in word and deed?[24]

One only needs to remember what Eusebius praises about the apostolic leaders of the church—their humility, poverty, and unrelenting commitment to the gospel—to understand why Paul would have so offended him and others in the church. In the end, the council removed Paul from his ministry, and Paul "lost both the orthodoxy of his faith and his bishopric."[25]

Eusebius concludes the first edition of his *History* by claiming that he had covered the "successions from the Savior's birth," from the earliest successors of the apostles down to his own day in the late third century.[26] Certain of the church's faith in the face of all opposition—both earthly and demonic—Eusebius portrays a victorious church that is the latest chapter in a very ancient story about God's involvement in human history.

DISCUSSION QUESTIONS

1. Eusebius connects the historical transmission of the teaching of the apostles, the historical transmission of the authority of bishops, and the canon of the New Testament. How and why does he do that? Is this a helpful way to define the church for you?

2. Eusebius found the record of how Christians responded during the plague in Egypt inspiring. What did Christians do? Can you think of examples of Christians responding to tragedies like that in the contemporary world?

3. The episode of Paul of Samosata is important to Eusebius as an example of the church defining itself against false teaching. Who was Paul of Samosata and why was he removed from his position of authority? Does the episode involving him remind of you of any contemporary problems with Christian leaders? How should contemporary Christians respond to a crisis of leadership like the one the church in Antioch faced in the third century?

What to Read Next

There are many excellent books about early Christianity, and this section will highlight a few that you could read if you want to learn more about Christianity in the Roman Empire. Though they all cover the period AD 100–300 (the time frame for this book), some of these titles include material beyond the year 300. The complete bibliography follows the notes.

GENERAL BOOKS

Chadwick, Henry. *The Early Church*. Rev. ed. New York and London: Penguin Books, 1993.

Chadwick was a distinguished historian of early Christianity in the twentieth century. This is his classic survey of early Christianity.

Driver, Lisa D. Maugans. *Christ at the Center: The Early Christian Era*. Louisville, KY: Westminster John Knox, 2009.

In this introduction to the theology of early Christians, Driver focuses on how the development of the Christian church as a worshiping community influenced their understanding of God and Christ.

Litfin, Bryan M. *Getting to Know the Church Fathers*. 2nd ed. Grand Rapids, MI: Baker Academic, 2016.

Intended to be accessible for general readers, Litfin's book is a collection of biographies of early Christian figures, some of which are discussed in this book.

BOOKS ON PART I

The Apostolic Fathers in English. 3rd ed. Edited and revised by Michael W. Holmes. Grand Rapids, MI: Baker, 2006.

Michael Holmes is an expert on the Apostolic Fathers, and this volume is an accessible and readable translation of these texts.

Jefford, Clayton N. *Reading the Apostolic Fathers*. 2nd ed. Grand Rapids, MI: Baker Academic, 2012.

Jefford's book is an excellent introduction to the Apostolic Fathers and is intended for a wide audience of readers.

BOOKS ON PART II

Grant, Robert. *Greek Apologists of the Second Century*. Philadelphia, PA: The Westminster Press, 1988.

Another distinguished twentieth-century scholar of early Christianity, Grant wrote many books on early Christianity. This book is his classic study of the apologists.

Litfin, Bryan. *Early Christian Martyr Stories*. Grand Rapids, MI: Baker, 2014.

Like in his book on the church fathers noted above, Litfin follows a biographical approach in this study of the persecution of Christians. He covers the martyrdom accounts of some of the figures discussed in this book.

Wilkin, Robert L. *The Christians as the Romans Saw Them*. New Haven, CT: Yale University Press, 1984.

This is a great source for those interested in learning more about Roman observers and critics of Christianity in the Roman Empire, including Pliny and Trajan and Celsus.

BOOKS ON PART III

Dunn, Geoffrey D. *Tertullian*. The Early Church Fathers. London and New York: Routledge, 2004.

Grant, Robert M. *Irenaeus of Lyons*. The Early Church Fathers. London and New York: Routledge, 1996.

Stewart-Sykes, Alistair. *Melito of Sardis: On Pascha*. Popular Patristics Series 20. Crestwood, NY: St. Vladimir's Seminary Press, 2001.

Trigg, Joseph. *Origen*. The Early Church Fathers. London and New York: Routledge, 1998.

Notes

CHAPTER 1

1. For the English translation and a helpful discussion of the Priene inscription, see Craig A. Evans, "Mark's Incipit and the Priene Calendar Inscription: From Jewish Gospel to Greco-Roman Gospel," *Journal of Greco-Roman Christianity and Judaism* 1 (2000): 67–81.

2. William H. C. Frend, *The Rise of Christianity* (Philadelphia, PA: Fortress Press, 1984), 150.

3. Tacitus, *Annals* XV.44 [English: Ronald Mellor, *The Historians of Ancient Rome*, 2nd ed. (New York: Routledge, 2004), 514].

4. Tacitus, *Annals* XV.44 [English: Ronald Mellor, *The Historians of Ancient Rome*, 2nd ed. (New York: Routledge, 2004), 513].

5. Eusebius of Caesarea, a Christian historian of the late third and early fourth centuries, claims in his *Ecclesiastical History* that Domitian demonstrated "appalling cruelty" toward Roman elites he found suspicious and toward Christians and Jews. Eusebius, *Ecclesiastical History* III.17–20 [English: *The History of the Church*, trans. G. A. Williamson (Penguin, 1989), 80–82].

6. On the question of Domitian's relationship with Jews and Christians, see Brian W. Jones, *The Emperor Domitian* (New York: Routledge, 1993), 114–19.

7. He was called the "the Younger" to differentiate him from his uncle Pliny the Elder, a noted historian and author of the mid to late first century.

8. Pliny, "Letters 10.96" [English: *Pliny the Younger: Complete Letters*, trans. P. G. Walsh, Oxford World's Classics (Oxford, 2009), 278–79].

9. On this point see Robert Wilken, *Christians as the Romans Saw Them* (New Haven, CT: Yale University Press, 1984), 21–25.

10. See again Wilken, *Christians as the Romans Saw Them*, 8–15.

11. Pliny, "Letters 10.96" [English: *Pliny the Younger: Complete Letters*, 278–79].

12. On the judicial torture of slaves, see Keith Bradley, *Slavery and Society of Rome* (Cambridge: Cambridge University Press, 1994), 165–70.

CHAPTER 2

1. Pliny, "Letter 10:96" [English: *Pliny the Younger: Complete Letters*, trans. P. G. Walsh, Oxford World's Classics (Oxford, 2009), 278–79].

2. *Didache* 1.1 [English: *The Apostolic Fathers*, 3rd ed., trans. and ed. Michael W. Holmes (Grand Rapids, MI: Baker Academic, 2006), 163].

3. See chapter five for the *Didache* on Christian worship and church order.

4. See Clayton N. Jefford, *Reading the Apostolic Fathers* (Peabody, MA: Hendrickson Publishers, 1996), 11–51.

5. *Didache* 1.2 [English: *The Apostolic Fathers*, 163].

6. *Didache* 2.1 [English: *The Apostolic Fathers*, 164].

7. On the unique sexual ethic Christianity required of its adherents, see Larry Hurtado, *Destroyer of the Gods: Early Christian Distinctiveness in the Roman World* (Waco, TX: Baylor University Press, 2016), 154–68.

8. See John Gager, ed., *Curse Tablets and Binding Spells from the Ancient World* (Oxford, 1992), 78–115.

9. *Didache* 2.7 [English: *The Apostolic Fathers*, 164].

10. *Didache* 3.4–6 [English: *The Apostolic Fathers*, 164].

11. *Didache* 4.9–11 [English: *The Apostolic Fathers*, 165].

12. *Didache* 4.2–4 [English: *The Apostolic Fathers*, 165].

13. *Didache* 4.7–8 [English: *The Apostolic Fathers*, 165].

14. *Didache* 4.14 [English: *The Apostolic Fathers*, 165].

15. *Didache* 5.2 [English: *The Apostolic Fathers*, 166].

16. *Didache* 5.2 [English: *The Apostolic Fathers*, 166].

17. *The Epistle of Barnabas* 19.2, 19.5 [English: *The Apostolic Fathers*, 196].

18. *The Epistle of Barnabas* 19.5 [English: *The Apostolic Fathers*, 196].

19. *The Epistle of Barnabas* 19.7, 8 [English: *The Apostolic Fathers*, 196].

20. *The Epistle of Barnabas* 19.11 [English: *The Apostolic Fathers*, 197].

21. *The Epistle of Barnabas* 19.12 [English: *The Apostolic Fathers*, 197].

22. *The Epistle of Barnabas* 20.2 [English: *The Apostolic Fathers*, 197].

CHAPTER 3

1. *1 Clement* 1.1 [English: *The Apostolic Fathers*, 3rd ed., trans. and ed. Michael W. Holmes (Grand Rapids, MI: Baker Academic, 2006), 42].

2. See chapter one for more on Domitian's persecution. Note, however, that some scholars believe that Clement is referring to internal problems in the Roman church rather than to persecution. Nothing precludes it from being a reference to both.

3. *1 Clement* 7.2 [English: *The Apostolic Fathers*, 45].

4. *1 Clement* 7.4–7 [English: *The Apostolic Fathers*, 45–46].

5. *1 Clement* 42.1 [English: *The Apostolic Fathers*, 61].

6. *1 Clement* 16.2, 36.1 [English: *The Apostolic Fathers*, 49, 59].

7. *1 Clement* 49.6 [English: *The Apostolic Fathers*, 65]. Clayton Jefford has identified blood imagery in connection with Jesus's death for all and human salvation as a prominent theme of Clement's letter. (*Reading the Apostolic Fathers: An Introduction* [repr., Grand Rapids, MI: Baker Academic, 2012], 109).

8. *1 Clement* 58.1, 2 [English: *The Apostolic Fathers*, 69].

9. *1 Clement* 13.1–3 [English: *The Apostolic Fathers*, 48].

10. *1 Clement* 1.1 [English: *The Apostolic Fathers*, 42].

11. *1 Clement* 1.2–2.4 [English: *The Apostolic Fathers*, 42–43]. In her study of this letter, Barbara Bowe notes that the language Clement uses to praise the virtues and former unity the Corinthian church possessed, which he is also urging them to restore, is reminiscent of the rhetoric ancient orators used to praise the ideals of the ancient Roman family or a virtuous and united city-state. This shows that Clement not only drew on biblical models to persuade his audience but also models from his culture. See Bowe, *A Church in Crisis: Ecclesiology and Paraenesis in Clement of Rome* (Minneapolis: Fortress Press, 1988), 86–87, 97–103.

12. *1 Clement* 3.2–4 [English: *The Apostolic Fathers*, 43].

13. *1 Clement* 42.1–5 [English: *The Apostolic Fathers*, 61].

14. *1 Clement* 44.1–4 [English: *The Apostolic Fathers*, 62–63].

15. *1 Clement* 45.7 [English: *The Apostolic Fathers*, 63].

16. *1 Clement* 47.7 [English: *The Apostolic Fathers*, 64].

17. *1 Clement* 20.1–12 [English: *The Apostolic Fathers*, 52].

18. *1 Clement* 15.1 [English: *The Apostolic Fathers*, 49].

19. *1 Clement* 32.4–33.1 [English: *The Apostolic Fathers*, 56–57].

20. *1 Clement* 35.5 [English: *The Apostolic Fathers*, 58].

21. Another example is Suetonius [Sway-TONE-ee-us], a biographer of the emperors and also a contemporary of Pliny and Tacitus. In his biography of Nero he mentions Christians briefly: "Punishments were also inflicted on the Christians, a sect professing a new and mischievous religious belief." Suetonius, "Nero," *The Twelve Caesars*, trans. Robert Graves (London: Penguin Books, 1979), 221.

CHAPTER 4

1. As William R. Schoedel comments, "Unity may well represent the central theme of the letters of Ignatius." See Schoedel, *Ignatius of Antioch* (Philadelphia, PA: Fortress Press, 1985), 21.

2. Ignatius, *To the Magnesians* 3.1, 6.1 [English: *The Apostolic Fathers*, 3rd ed., trans. and ed. Michael W. Holmes (Grand Rapids, MI: Baker Academic, 2006), 104].

3. Ignatius, *To the Trallians* 3.1 [English: *The Apostolic Fathers*, 109].

4. Ignatius, *To the Ephesians* 4.1 and *To the Philadelphians* 3.2 [English: *The Apostolic Fathers*, 97, 118].

5. On this point see Gregory Vall, *Learning Christ* (Washington, DC: The Catholic University of America Press, 2013), 211.

6. Ignatius, *To the Magnesians* 7.2 [English: *The Apostolic Fathers*, 105].

7. Ignatius, *To the Magnesians* 8.1–2 [English: *The Apostolic Fathers*, 105].

8. Ignatius, *To the Magnesians* 9.1–2 [English: *The Apostolic Fathers*, 105].

9. Ignatius, *To the Magnesians* 9.2 [English: *The Apostolic Fathers*, 105].

10. Ignatius, *To the Philadelphians* 6.1 [English: *The Apostolic Fathers*, 107–8].

11. Ignatius, *To the Philadelphians* 8.2–9.1 [English: *The Apostolic Fathers*, 119–20].

12. Ignatius, *To the Ephesians* 7.2 [English: *The Apostolic Fathers*, 98].

13. Ignatius, *To the Smyrnaeans* 1.1–2 [English: *The Apostolic Fathers*, 121].

14. Ignatius, *To the Trallians* 9.1–2 [English: *The Apostolic Fathers*, 110].

15. Ignatius, *To the Trallians* 10.1 [English: *The Apostolic Fathers*, 110].

16. See for example 1 John 1:1–3 and 4:1–3

17. Ignatius, *To the Trallians* 6.1–2 [English: *The Apostolic Fathers*, 109–10].

18. Ignatius, *To the Ephesians* 7.1, 16.1–2 [English: *The Apostolic Fathers*, 98, 101].

19. Ignatius, *To the Trallians* 10.1, 11.1 and *To the Smyrnaeans* 5.3 [English: *The Apostolic Fathers*, 110–11, 122].

20. Ignatius, *To the Romans* 4.1–2 [English: *The Apostolic Fathers*, 114].

21. Ignatius, *To the Romans* 6.3 [English: *The Apostolic Fathers*, 115].

22. Ignatius, *To the Smyrnaeans* 4.2 [English: *The Apostolic Fathers*, 122].

23. Ignatius, *To the Smyrnaeans* 6.2 [English: *The Apostolic Fathers*, 123].

24. Ignatius, *To Polycarp* 3.2 [English: *The Apostolic Fathers*, 127].

25. Ignatius, *To Polycarp* 4.1, 3 and 5.1 [English: *The Apostolic Fathers*, 127].

CHAPTER 5

1. *Didache* 7.1-4 [English: *The Apostolic Fathers*, 3rd ed., trans. and ed. Michael W. Holmes (Grand Rapids, MI: Baker Academic, 2006), 166–67].

2. See Jefford, *Reading the Apostolic Fathers*, 48–49.

3. The baptistery is part of a small church building, a converted house, at Dura Europos, a Roman garrison town on the Euphrates river in modern Syria. For a full account, see Carl H. Kraeling, *The Christian Building: Dura Europas* (New Haven, CT: Yale University Press, 1967).

4. For example, see Romans 6. In the *The Epistle of Barnabas*, the author argues that Christian baptism is prefigured in the Old Testament (11.1–11 [English: *The Apostolic Fathers*, 189–90]). Ignatius of Antioch connects the baptism of Jesus and his crucifixion, claiming that both "purified the water," presumably to make it spiritually effective for future Christians (*To the Ephesians* 18.2 [English: *The Apostolic Fathers*, 101]).

5. The word that early Christians used for the Lord's Supper or communion was the Greek word *eucharistia*, literally the "thanksgiving." In this chapter I will use the word Eucharist when talking about how early Christians understood communion.

6. *Didache* 9.5 [English: *The Apostolic Fathers*, 168].

7. *Didache* 9.2 [English: *The Apostolic Father*, 167].

8. *Didache* 9.3–4 [English: *The Apostolic Father*, 168].

9. *Didache* 10.2 [English: *The Apostolic Fathers*, 168].

10. *Didache* 10.3 [English: *The Apostolic Fathers*, 168].

11. *Didache* 14.1–3 [English: *The Apostolic Fathers*, 170].

12. For this reading of *Didache* 14, see Jonathan A. Draper, "Pure Sacrifice in *Didache* 14 as Jewish Christian Exegesis," *Neotestamenica* 42.2 (2008): 223–52.

13. *1 Clement* 40.4 [English: *The Apostolic Fathers*, 61].

14. *1 Clement* 41.1 [English: *The Apostolic Fathers*, 61].

15. *To the Smyrnaeans* 6.2 [English: *The Apostolic Fathers*, 123].

16. *To the Philadelphians* 4.1 [English: *The Apostolic Fathers*, 118].

17. *To the Ephesians* 20.2 [English: *The Apostolic Fathers*, 102].

18. *To the Romans* 7.3 [English: *The Apostolic Fathers*, 115].

19. *Didache* 15.1–2 [English: *The Apostolic Fathers*, 170–71].

20. *Didache* 11.8 [English: *The Apostolic Fathers*, 169].

21. *Didache* 10.7 [English: *The Apostolic Fathers*, 169].

PART TWO

1. The two exceptions are the persecution of the emperor Decius (r. 249–51), which we will discuss in chapter ten, and the "Great Persecution" (303–11) initiated by the emperor Diocletian.

2. Lucian of Samosata, "Passing of Peregrinus 13" in *Lucian*, vol. 5, Loeb Classical Library 302 (Cambridge: Harvard University Press, 1936), 15.

CHAPTER 6

1. Scholars vary on the date of *The Epistle to Diognetus*. One theory places the author during the early second-century and under the reign of Emperor Hadrian (r. 117–38). An alternate theory suggests the author wrote during the late second century, perhaps as late as the 190s. For an account of the early date see Cyril C. Richardson, "The So-Called Letter to Diognetus," in *Early Christian Fathers*, reprint (New York: Touchstone, 1996), 206–10. For the later date, see Robert Grant, *Greek Apologists of the Second Century* (Philadelphia, PA: The Westminster Press, 1988), 178–79. Clayton Jefford's edition of the text is ambivalent, claiming the author wrote at some point in the mid to late second century. Jefford, *The Epistle to Diognetus (with the Fragment of Quadratus): Introduction, Text, and Commentary*, Oxford Apostolic Fathers (Oxford: Oxford University Press, 2013).

2. "*The Epistle to Diognetus* 2.4–6" [English: "The So-Called Letter to Diognetus," ed. and trans. Eugene R. Fairweather, in Cyril C. Richardson, *Early Christian Fathers*, Library of Christian Classics, vol. 1 reprint (New York: Touchstone, 1996), 214].

3. "*The Epistle to Diognetus* 2.10" [English: *Early Christian Fathers*, 215].

4. "*The Epistle to Diognetus* 4.1, 6" [English: *Early Christian Fathers*, 216].

5. "*The Epistle to Diognetus* 4.6" [English: *Early Christian Fathers*, 216].

6. "*The Epistle to Diognetus* 1" [English: *Early Christian Fathers*, 213].

7. "*The Epistle to Diognetus* 5.1–15, 6.1–3" [English: *Early Christian Fathers*, 216–18].

8. "*The Epistle to Diognetus* 6.4–10" [English: *Early Christian Fathers*, 218].

9. "*The Epistle to Diognetus* 7.2, 4" [English: *Early Christian Fathers*, 218–19].

10. "*The Epistle to Diognetus* 9.2–3" [English: *Early Christian Fathers*, 220–21].

11. On the author's presentation of the role of the Son of God and God's plan for human salvation, see Michael Heintz, "MIMETES THEOU in the Epistle of Diognetus," *Journal of Early Christian Studies* 12.1 (2004): 111–17.

12. Celsus, *On the True Doctrine*, trans. R. Joseph Hoffman (Oxford, 1987), 74. As Hoffman points out, this is similar to the description Paul gives of what the Corinthian Christians used to be like before their conversion in 1 Corinthians 6:9–11 [*On the True Doctrine*, 134–67].

13. *On the True Doctrine*, 73.

14. *On the True Doctrine*, 77.

15. *On the True Doctrine*, 116–120.

16. *On the True Doctrine*, 78.

17. *On the True Doctrine*, 107.

18. *On the True Doctrine*, 108.

19. *On the True Doctrine*, 108.

20. *On the True Doctrine*, 105.

21. *On the True Doctrine*, 122.

CHAPTER 7

1. Justin Martyr, *Dialogue with Trypho* 1–9.

2. Justin Martyr, *First Apology* 1–2 [English: *St. Justin Martyr: The First and Second Apologies*, trans. Leslie William Barnard, Ancient Christian Writers (Mahwah, NJ: Paulist Press, 1997), 23].

3. *First Apology* 3 [English: *St. Justin Martyr*, 24].

4. *First Apology* 4 [English: *St. Justin Martyr*, 25].

5. *First Apology* 5 [English: *St. Justin Martyr*, 25].

6. *First Apology* 5 [English: *St. Justin Martyr*, 26].

7. *First Apology* 9–10 [English: *St. Justin Martyr*, 27–28].

8. *First Apology* 12 [English: *Justin Martyr*, 29].

9. *First Apology* 12 [English: *Justin Martyr*, 29].

10. *First Apology* 17 [English: *Justin Martyr*, 29, 34–35].

11. *First Apology* 15–16 [English: *Justin Martyr*, 29, 32–34].

12. *First Apology* 13 [English: *Justin Martyr*, 31]. In the second century, Christians had not settled on the best language to use to describe the mystery of God as Trinity. Although Justin's language of "rank" or "place" may sound odd to the ears of contemporary Christians, this was a typical way to express belief about the Trinity among early Christians.

13. *First Apology* 23 [English: *Justin Martyr*, 39].

14. *First Apology* 22 [English: *Justin Martyr*, 39]. In Greek mythology, Perseus's mother, Danae, was impregnated by Zeus without any sexual union between the two of them, thus conceiving Perseus as a virgin. Asclepius was a famed physician who eventually was elevated to the god of healing.

15. *First Apology* 24 [English: *Justin Martyr*, 39–40].

16. *First Apology* 25 [English: *Justin Martyr*, 40].

17. *First Apology* 27 [English: *Justin Martyr*, 41–42].

18. *First Apology* 28 [English: *Justin Martyr*, 42].

19. *First Apology* 31 [English: *Justin Martyr*, 44].

20. *First Apology* 46 [English: *Justin Martyr*, 55].

21. *First Apology* 59 [English: *Justin Martyr*, 64–65].

22. Justin did not invent this idea that Greek philosophers, such as Plato, got their ideas from the older prophets of Israel. Justin may have taken this idea over from a first century Jewish writer named Philo, a contemporary of Jesus and Paul, who drew on Greek philosophy to argue in favor of Judaism. See Bruce Chilton, "Justin and Israelite Prophecy," in Sara Parvis and Paul Foster, eds., *Justin Martyr and His Worlds* (Minneapolis: Fortress Press, 2007), 81–82.

23. *First Apology* 54 [English: *Justin Martyr*, 61].

24. *First Apology* 61 [English: *Justin Martyr*, 66].

25. Isaiah 1:16–20; *First Apology* 61 [English: *Justin Martyr*, 66–67].

26. *First Apology* 66 [English: *Justin Martyr*, 70].

27. Sara Parvis argues that the reason for this continuity is that Justin was a trail-blazer and other Christians, realizing the power and poignancy of what he had written, self-consciously imitated his approach. In essence, Justin invented the genre of Christian apology. Sara Parvis, "Justin Martyr and the Apologetic Tradition," in Sara Parvis and Paul Foster, eds., *Justin Martyr and His Worlds* (Minneapolis: Fortress Press, 2007), 115–27.

CHAPTER 8

1. Pliny, "Letter 10.96" [English: *Pliny the Younger: Complete Letters*, trans. P. G. Walsh, Oxford World's Classics (Oxford, 2009), 278].

2. Pliny, "Letter 10.96" [English: *Pliny the Younger: Complete Letters*, trans. P. G. Walsh, Oxford World's Classics (Oxford, 2009), 278–79].

3. See Wilken, *The Christians as the Romans Saw Them*, 22–29.

4. Trajan, preserved in Pliny, "Letter 10.97" [English: *Pliny the Younger: Complete Letters*, 279].

5. *The Martyrdom of Polycarp* 1.2 [English: "Martyrdom of Polycarp," trans. Massey Hamilton Shepherd, in *Early Christian Fathers*, ed. Cyril C. Richardson (New York: Simon and Schuster, 1996), 149].

6. *The Martyrdom of Polycarp* 4 [English: *Early Christian Fathers*, 150].

7. *The Martyrdom of Polycarp* 3.2 [English: *Early Christian Fathers*, 150].

8. *The Martyrdom of Polycarp* 9.2–10.2 [English: *Early Christian Fathers*, 150–51].

9. *The Martyrdom of Polycarp* 12.1–3 [English: *Early Christian Fathers*, 153–54].

CHAPTER 9

1. *The Martyrdom of Perpetua and Felicity* 21 [English: "The Martyrdom of Perpetua," trans. Rosemary Rader, in *A Lost Tradition: Women Writers of the Early Church*, eds. Patricia Wilson-Kastner, et al. (Washington, DC: University Press of America, 1981), 30].

2. *The Martyrdom of Perpetua and Felicity* 2 [English: *A Lost Tradition*, 19–20].

3. There have been a number of theories about Perpetua's husband including that he had died recently, that he was a timid Christian in hiding, and that he was travelling far from Carthage. For these theories and her own unique interpretation that Saturus is Perpetua's husband, see Carolyn Osiek, "Perpetua's Husband," *Journal of Early Christian Studies* 10.2 (Summer 2002): 287–90. Was her husband a pagan who had denounced her to the authorities and abandoned her? This also seems to be a possibility. Brent Shaw is convinced, at the very least, that he was a pagan hostile to Perpetua's Christian faith. Shaw, "The Passion of Perpetua," *Past and Present* 139 (May 1993): 24–25.

4. *The Martyrdom of Perpetua and Felicity* 3 [English: *A Lost Tradition*, 20].

5. *The Martyrdom of Perpetua and Felicity* 5 [English: *A Lost Tradition*, 21–22].

6. For a discussion on the status of Perpetua and her family and on her relationship with her father, see Thomas J. Heffernan, *The Passion of Perpetua* (Oxford: Oxford University Press, 2012), 28–46.

7. On the other hand, Thomas J. Heffernan argues that Revocatus, another slave who is martyred and is mentioned in tandem with Felicity, may have been from the same house and may be her partner (Roman law did not recognize the marriages of slaves) and the father of her child. See Heffernan, *The Passion of Perpetua*, 19–20.

8. *The Martyrdom of Perpetua and Felicity* 15 [English: *A Lost Tradition*, 26].

9. *The Martyrdom of Perpetua and Felicity* 15 [English: *A Lost Tradition*, 27].

10. *The Martyrdom of Perpetua and Felicity* 1 [English: *A Lost Tradition*, 19].

11. *The Martyrdom of Perpetua and Felicity* 4 [English: *A Lost Tradition*, 21].

12. *The Martyrdom of Perpetua and Felicity* 10 [English: *A Lost Tradition*, 24–25].

13. *The Martyrdom of Perpetua and Felicity* 18 [English: *A Lost Tradition*, 28].

14. *The Martyrdom of Perpetua and Felicity* 13 [English: *A Lost Tradition*, 26].

CHAPTER 10

1. The church historian Eusebius of Caesarea, writing in the 290s, claimed that Philip was a Christian [Eusebius, *Ecclesiastical History* VI.34]. See chapter fifteen for an account of Eusebius of Caesarea's history.

2. W. H. C. Frend, *The Rise of Christianity* (Philadelphia, PA: Fortress Press, 1984), 320–21.

3. Dionysius, "Letter to Fabius," in Eusebius of Caesarea, *Ecclesiastical History* VI.41 [English: *The History of the Church*, trans. G. A. Williamson (Penguin, 1989), 211].

4. Dionysius, "Letter to Fabius," in Eusebius of Caesarea, *Ecclesiastical History* VI.41 [English: *The History of the Church*, trans. G. A. Williamson (Penguin, 1989), 211–12].

5. Cyprian, *On the Lapsed* 8, 9 [English: *St. Cyprian: The Lapsed, On the Unity of the Catholic Church*, trans. Maurice Bevenot, Ancient Christian Writers (Mahwah, NJ: Paulist Press, 1957), 19–20].

6. Cyprian, *On the Lapsed* 10 [English: *St. Cyprian*, 21].

7. Cyprian, *On the Lapsed* 11 [English: *St. Cyprian*, 21].

8. The English word priest comes from the ancient Greek word *presbyter*, which appears in the New Testament. It is often translated as "elder."

9. Keep in mind that the word "Catholic" here is not a word indicating a particular branch of Christianity as it is today. Among ancient Christians, the phrase "catholic church" meant the church that represented what all Christians everywhere believed and the church that had faithfully maintained the teaching of the apostles and the Bible generation after generation.

10. Cyprian, *On the Unity of the Catholic Church* 6 [English: *St. Cyprian*, 48–49].

11. Cyprian, *On the Unity of the Catholic Church* 6 [English: *St. Cyprian*, 48].

12. Cyprian, *On the Unity of the Catholic Church* 5 [English: *St. Cyprian*, 47].

13. Cyprian, *On the Unity of the Catholic Church* 5 [English: *St. Cyprian*, 47–48].

14. Cyprian, *On the Unity of the Catholic Church* 7 [English: *St. Cyprian*, 49].

15. Cyprian, *On the Unity of the Catholic Church* 3 [English: *St. Cyprian*, 45].

16. Cyprian, *On the Unity of the Catholic Church* 10 [English: *St. Cyprian*, 53].

17. Cyprian, *On the Unity of the Catholic Church* 13 [English: *St. Cyprian*, 56].

18. As Brent Allen has observed, Cyprian has a difficult problem here. Those about to be martyred or who were suffering for their faith had for a long time held a special status within the North African church and elsewhere. There was a tradition of them granting forgiveness or reconciliation. In a sense, Cyprian's solution to claim that only a bishop has the authority to reconcile the lapsed to the church is more of an innovation than what Felicissimus and the confessors were doing [Allen, *Cyprian and Roman Carthage* (Cambridge: Cambridge University Press, 2010), 253–73].

19. Cyprian, *On the Unity of the Catholic Church* 21 [English: *St. Cyprian*, 63–64].

20. Cyprian, *On the Unity of the Catholic Church* 22 [English: *St. Cyprian*, 64].

PART THREE

1. From the title of chapter eight, "Out of the Shadows: 193–235" of W. H. C. Frend, *The Rise of Christianity*, 271.

2. Eusebius of Caesarea recounts an episode involving Christians arguing over church property. The Roman emperor Aurelian (r. 270–75) issued a decision on the case. It is worth noting that there was no persecution of the Christians following this episode, though Aurelian apparently was considering a persecution before he died. See Eusebius of Caesarea, *Ecclesiastical History* VII.30 [English: *The History of the Church*, trans. G. A. Williamson (Penguin, 1989), 248].

CHAPTER 11

1. Following the dating analysis of Alistair Stewart-Sykes in *Melito of Sardis: On Pascha* (Crestwood, NY: St. Vladimir's Seminary Press, 2001), 1.

2. Stewart-Sykes, *Melito of Sardis: On Pascha*, 3.

3. Melito, *Extracts*, "Introduction," in Eusebius of Caesarea, *Ecclesiastical History* IV.26.12–14 [English: Eusebius, *The History of the Church*, trans. G. A. Williamson (London: Penguin Classics, 1989), 135].

4. *On the Passover* 2 [English: *Melito of Sardis: On Pascha*, 37].

5. *On the Passover* 4–5 [English: *Melito of Sardis: On Pascha*, 38].

6. Frances Young, *Biblical Exegesis and the Formation of Christian Culture* (Cambridge: Cambridge University Press, 1997), 193.

7. *On the Passover* 33 [English: *Melito of Sardis: On Pascha*, 45].

8. Young, *Biblical Exegesis*, 195.

9. *On the Passover* 36–37 [English: *Melito of Sardis: On Pascha*, 46].

10. *On the Passover* 39–42 [English: *Melito of Sardis: On Pascha*, 47].

11. *On First Principles* IV.1 [English: "On First Principles: Book IV," in *Origen*, trans. Rowan Greer, Classics of Western Spirituality (Mahwah, NJ: Paulist Press, 1979), 171–78]. On Origen's view on the inspiration and inerrancy of the Bible, see Michael Holmes, "Origen and the Inerrancy of Scripture," *Journal of the Evangelical Theological Society* 24.3 (September 1981): 221–31.

12. *On First Principles* IV.1.7 [English: "On First Principles: Book IV," 176–78].

13. *On First Principles* IV.2.7 [English: "On First Principles: Book IV," 186].

14. *On First Principles* IV.2.8 [English: "On First Principles: Book IV," 187].

15. *On First Principles* IV.4.4 [English: "On First Principles: Book IV," 192].

16. *On First Principles* IV.2.6 and IV.3.8 [English: "On First Principles: Book IV," 184–85, 195–96]. In 1 Corinthians 10, Paul discusses the spiritual meaning of the Israelites in the wilderness. In Galatians 4, Paul argues that Isaac and Ishmael are figures for the earthly Jerusalem and the heavenly Jerusalem. Also see Robert Wilken, *The Spirit of Early Christian Thought* (New Haven, CT: Yale University Press, 2003), 69–72.

17. *On First Principles* IV.2.1–2 [English: "On First Principles: Book IV," 178–81].

CHAPTER 12

1. *Proof of the Apostolic Preaching* 1 [English: Irenaeus of Lyons, *Proof of the Apostolic Preaching*, trans. Joseph P. Smith (New York: Paulist Press, 1992), 47].

2. This is the claim of Eusebius of Caesarea in his discussion of Irenaeus. See Eusebius, *Ecclesiastical History* V.26 [English: *The History of the Church*, trans. G. A. Williamson (Penguin, 1989), 174].

3. *Proof of the Apostolic Preaching* 1 [English: *Proof of the Apostolic Preaching*, 47].

4. *Proof of the Apostolic Preaching* 1 [English: *Proof of the Apostolic Preaching*, 47].

5. *Proof of the Apostolic Preaching* 1 [English: *Proof of the Apostolic Preaching*, 47].

6. *Proof of the Apostolic Preaching* 6 [English: *Proof of the Apostolic Preaching*, 51].

7. *Proof of the Apostolic Preaching* 99 [English: *Proof of the Apostolic Preaching*, 108].

8. *Proof of the Apostolic Preaching* 5 [English: *Proof of the Apostolic Preaching*, 50].

9. *Proof of the Apostolic Preaching* 6 [English: *Proof of the Apostolic Preaching*, 51].

10. *Proof of the Apostolic Preaching* 7 [English: *Proof of the Apostolic Preaching*, 51].

11. *Proof of the Apostolic Preaching* 10 [English: *Proof of the Apostolic Preaching*, 54].

12. *Proof of the Apostolic Preaching* 4 [English: *Proof of the Apostolic Preaching*, 50].

13. Denis Minns argues that the heretics' belief that the highest God was not the creator God "preoccupied the attention of Irenaeus more than any other issue." See Minns, *Irenaeus: an Introduction* (London: T & T Clark, 2010), 33.

14. *Proof of the Apostolic Preaching* 11 [English: *Proof of the Apostolic Preaching*, 54].

15. *Proof of the Apostolic Preaching* 12 [English: *Proof of the Apostolic Preaching*, 55].

16. For Melito and Origen, see chapter eleven.

17. *Proof of the Apostolic Preaching* 21 [English: *Proof of the Apostolic Preaching*, 60]. Quotation of Genesis 9:27 is from the NRSV.

18. *Proof of the Apostolic Preaching* 25 [English: *Proof of the Apostolic Preaching*, 64]. This is similar to Melito of Sardis's reading of the Passover story. Irenaeus and Melito were almost exact contemporaries and lived in two different parts of the Roman Empire. It is unlikely that one influenced the other on this point. What we are observing in their similarities is a widespread Christian interpretation of the Passover, influenced by the New Testament.

19. The Greek version of the Old Testament, which most early Christians used, uses a Greek name that can be rendered as "Joshua" or "Jesus." Many early Christian writers were eager to make the kind of connections that Irenaeus does here, arguing that Joshua's virtues foreshadow Jesus Christ.

20. *Proof of the Apostolic Preaching* 27 [English: *Proof of the Apostolic Preaching*, 65].

21. *Proof of the Apostolic Preaching* 32 [English: *Proof of the Apostolic Preaching*, 68].

22. *Proof of the Apostolic Preaching* 32 [English: *Proof of the Apostolic Preaching*, 68].

23. See Eric Osborn, *Irenaeus of Lyons* (Cambridge: Cambridge University Press, 2001), 118–21.

24. *Proof of the Apostolic Preaching* 34 [English: *Proof of the Apostolic Preaching*, 69].

25. *Proof of the Apostolic Preaching* 39–40 [English: *Proof of the Apostolic Preaching*, 73].

26. *Proof of the Apostolic Preaching* 42 [English: *Proof of the Apostolic Preaching*, 75].

27. *Proof of the Apostolic Preaching* 52 [English: *Proof of the Apostolic Preaching*, 81].

28. *Proof of the Apostolic Preaching* 66 [English: *Proof of the Apostolic Preaching*, 90].

29. Such as Isaiah 7:14–16, Isaiah 9:6, and Isaiah 11:1–10.

30. *Proof of the Apostolic Preaching* 98 [English: *Proof of the Apostolic Preaching*, 108].

CHAPTER 13

1. On this point, see Johannes Quasten, *Patrology II: The Ante-Nicene Literature after Irenaeus* (Allen, TX: Christian Classics, 1986), 270–73.

2. See chapters eleven (Origen of Alexandria) and twelve (Irenaeus of Lyons).

3. *On the Flesh of Christ* 1 [English: *Tertullian's Treatise on the Incarnation*, trans. Ernest Evans (London: SPCK, 1956), 5].

4. As we read in the previous chapter, Irenaeus of Lyons also wrote against this heresy in his *Against the Heresies* and *Proof of the Apostolic Preaching*.

5. *On the Flesh of Christ* 2 [English: *Treatise on the Incarnation*, 7].

6. *On the Flesh of Christ* 5 [English: *Treatise on the Incarnation*, 17].

7. *On the Flesh of Christ* 5 [English: *Treatise on the Incarnation*, 17].

8. *On the Flesh of Christ* 5 [English: *Treatise on the Incarnation*, 19].

9. On the role that Mary plays in Tertullian's understanding of Christ's humanity, see Willemien Otten, "Christ's Birth of a Virgin Who Became a Wife: Flesh and Speech in Tertullian's 'De carne Christi,'" *Vigiliae Christianae* 51.3 (1997): 247–60.

10. *On the Flesh of Christ* 17 [English: *Treatise on the Incarnation*, 59].

11. *On the Flesh of Christ* 17 [English: *Treatise on the Incarnation*, 61].

12. Irenaeus of Lyons (see chapter eleven), an older contemporary of Tertullian, also drew these parallels between Mary and Eve. Tertullian may have derived his language here from Irenaeus, but it is equally possible that both of them are drawing on an idea that was already circulating among Christians.

13. J. N. D. Kelly, *Early Christian Doctrines*, rev. ed. (HarperSanFrancisco, 1978), 150–51.

CHAPTER 14

1. *Didache* 8.2–3, 15.4 [English: *The Apostolic Fathers*, 3rd ed., trans. and ed. Michael W. Holmes (Grand Rapids, MI: Baker Academic, 2006), 167, 171].

2. Hippolytus, *On the Apostolic Tradition* 41.1 [English: *On the Apostolic Tradition*, trans. Alistair Stewart-Sykes (Crestwood, NY: St. Vladimir's Seminary Press, 2001), 164].

3. *On the Apostolic Tradition* 41.1 [English: *On the Apostolic Tradition*, 164–65].

4. *On the Apostolic Tradition* 41.5–10 [English: *On the Apostolic Tradition*, 165]. Alistair Stewart-Sykes comments: "*Apostolic Tradition* is perhaps the first appearance of a cycle of daily prayer which is found commonly in later centuries, with prayer in the morning and evening supplemented by prayer three times in the day, and prayer at midnight added." Stewart-Sykes, *On the Apostolic Tradition*, 171.

5. *On the Apostolic Tradition* 41.18 [English: *On the Apostolic Tradition*, 166].

6. *On the Apostolic Tradition* 41.2 [English: *On the Apostolic Tradition*, 164]. It may be that this is a reference to catechetical instruction (instruction for those intending to be baptized and join the church) rather than a weekday system of "adult Christian education," but Hippolytus seems to assume that those already baptized will be present as well. There are references to other churches outside of Rome having these kinds of daily instructional times. See Paul Bradshaw et al., "Other Acts of Worship," *Essays on Hippolytus* (Bramcotte, UK: Grove Press, 1978), 62.

7. *On the Apostolic Tradition* 41.3 [English: *On the Apostolic Tradition*, 164].

8. *On Prayer* 2.1 [English: "On Prayer", in *Origen*, trans. Rowan Greer, Classics of Western Spirituality (Mahwah, NJ: Paulist Press, 1979), 82].

9. *On Prayer* 2.2 [English: *Origen*, 83].

10. *On Prayer* 2.5 [English: *Origen*, 86].

11. *On Prayer* 2.4 [English: *Origen*, 85].

12. Joseph Wilson Trigg, *Origen: The Bible and Philosophy in the Third-Century Church* (Atlanta, GA: John Knox Press, 1983), 159.

13. *On Prayer* 2.5 [English: *Origen*, 86].

14. *On Prayer* 2.5 [English: *Origen*, 86].

15. *On Prayer* 27.3 [English: *Origen*, 86].

16. *On Prayer* 31.2 [English: *Origen*, 164].

17. *On Prayer* 31.2 [English: *Origen*, 164–65].
18. *On Prayer* 31.3 [English: *Origen*, 165].
19. *On Prayer* 31.4 [English: *Origen*, 166].
20. *On Prayer* 31.4 [English: *Origen*, 166].
21. *On Prayer* 31.5 [English: *Origen*, 167].
22. *On Prayer* 31.5 [English: *Origen*, 166–67].
23. *On Prayer* 31.6 [English: *Origen*, 167]. Origen has in mind Isaiah 1:12–15.
24. *On Prayer* 32 [English: *Origen*, 168].

CHAPTER 15

1. Timothy Barnes has argued persuasively that Books 1–7 of Eusebius's history represents the original edition that he wrote in the 290s. See T. D. Barnes, *Constantine and Eusebius* (Cambridge, MA: Harvard University Press), 126–47.

2. Ancient authors often divided their longer works into sections they called "Books." We would call them chapters today.

3. Eusebius of Caesarea, *Ecclesiastical History* I.3 [English: *The History of the Church*, trans. G. A. Williamson (Penguin, 1989), 9–13].

4. Eusebius of Caesarea, *Ecclesiastical History* I.4 [English: *The History of the Church*, 16].

5. Ignatius of Antioch: *Ecclesiastical History* III.36 [English: *The History of the Church*, 97–100]; Clement of Rome: *Ecclesiastical History* III.37 [English: *The History of the Church*, 100].

6. Eusebius, *Ecclesiastical History* III.37 [English: *The History of the Church*, 100].

7. Polycarp: *Ecclesiastical History* IV.14–15 [English: *The History of the Church*, 116–23].

8. Justin Martyr: *Ecclesiastical History* IV.8–9, 11–13, 16–18 [English: *The History of the Church*, 111–12, 114–16, 123–28].

9. Melito of Sardis: *Ecclesiastical History* IV.26 [English: *The History of the Church*, 133–35]; Irenaeus of Lyon: *Ecclesiastical History* V.5–8, 20, 26 [English: *The History of the Church*, 152–56, 168–69, 174].

10. Eusebius, *Ecclesiastical History* VI.1–39 [English: *The History of the Church*, 179–209].

11. Eusebius, *Ecclesiastical History* III.3 [English: *The History of the Church*, 66].

12. Eusebius admits that there was some debate among Christians over James, 2 Peter, 2 and 3 John, Jude, and Revelation. The concern over these books was not their teaching; the concern was whether it was absolutely certain that these books were written by an apostle or not. In fact, Eusebius himself was not convinced that the apostle Peter wrote 2 Peter. See Eusebius, *Ecclesiastical History* III.3, III.24–25 [English: *The History of the Church*, trans. G. A. Williamson (Penguin, 1989), 65–66, 86–89].

13. Eusebius, *Ecclesiastical History* II.13 [English: *The History of the Church*, 48].

14. Eusebius, *Ecclesiastical History* VII.22 [English: *The History of the Church*, 237].

15. Rodney Stark, *The Rise of Christianity* (HarperSanFrancisco, 1997), 73.

16. Eusebius, *Ecclesiastical History* VII.22 [English: *The History of the Church*, 237].

17. Eusebius, *Ecclesiastical History* VII.22 [English: *The History of the Church*, 237].

18. Eusebius, *Ecclesiastical History* VII.22 [English: *The History of the Church*, 237].

19. Rodney Stark, *The Rise of Christianity*, 82–93.

20. Eusebius, *Ecclesiastical History* VII.27 [English: *The History of the Church*, 244].

21. Eusebius, *Ecclesiastical History* VII.30 [English: *The History of the Church*, 246].

22. Apparently the council did provide these details, but Eusebius did not include this part of the letter in his history. For more on "adoptionism," see J. N. D. Kelly, *Early Christian Doctrines*, rev. ed. (New York: HarperCollins, 1978), 109–24. For a more detailed discussion of Paul of Samosata and the synod of Antioch, see John Behr, *The Formation of Christian Theology I: The Way to Nicaea* (New York: St. Vladimir's Seminary Press, 2001), 207–35.

23. A *ducenarius* was a generic term for a Roman official who had the wealth of someone in the upper class of a city.

24. Eusebius, *Ecclesiastical History* VII.30 [English: *The History of the Church*, 246–47].

25. Eusebius, Ecclesiastical History VII.30 [English: *The History of the Church*, 248].

26. Eusebius, *Ecclesiastical History* VII.32 [English: *The History of the Church*, 255].

Bibliography

ANCIENT TEXTS

The Apostolic Fathers in English. 3rd ed. Translated and edited by Michael W. Holmes. Grand Rapids, MI: Baker Academic, 2006.

Celsus. *On the True Doctrine.* Translated by R. Joseph Hoffman. Oxford: Oxford University Press, 1997.

Cyprian of Carthage. *On the Unity of the Catholic Church.* Translated by Maurice Bevenot. Ancient Christian Writers 25. New York: The Newman Press, 1956.

The Epistle to Diognetus. Edited and Translated by Eugene R. Fairweather. In Richardson, *Early Christian Fathers.*

Eusebius of Caesarea. *The History of the Church.* Translated by G. A. Williamson. Revised and edited by Andrew Louth. New York: Penguin Books, 1989.

Hippolytus. *On the Apostolic Tradition.* Translated by Alistair Stewart-Sykes. Crestwood, NY: St. Vladimir's Seminary Press, 2001.

Irenaeus of Lyons. *Proof of the Apostolic Preaching.* Translated by Joseph P. Smith. Ancient Christian Writers 16. Mahwah, NJ: Paulist Press, 1992.

Justin Martyr. *First Apology.* Translated by Leslie William Barnard. Ancient Christian Writers 56. New York: The Newman Press, 1997.

Lucian of Samosata. *Passing of Peregrinus.* In vol. 5 of *Lucian.* Translated by A. M. Harmon. Loeb Classical Library 302. Cambridge, MA: Harvard University Press, 1936.

The Martyrdom of Perpetua and Felicity. Translated by Rosemary Rader. In Patricia Wilson-Kastner, et al. *A Lost Tradition: Women Writers of the Early Church.* Washington, DC: University Press of America, 1981.

"Martyrdom of Polycarp." Edited and translated by Eugene R. Fair-weather. In Richardson, *Early Christian Fathers*.

Melito of Sardis. *On Pascha*. Translated by Alistair Stewart-Sykes. Crestwood, NY: St. Vladimir's Seminary Press, 2001.

Origen of Alexandria. "On First Principles: IV." In *Origen*. Translated by Rowan Greer. Classics of Western Spirituality. Mahwah, NJ: Paulist Press, 1979.

————. "On Prayer." In *Origen*. Translated by Rowan Greer. Classics of Western Spirituality. Mahwah, NJ: Paulist Press, 1979.

Pliny. *Pliny the Younger: Complete Letters*. Translated by P. G. Walsh. Oxford World's Classics. Oxford: Oxford University Press, 2009.

Richardson, Cyril C. *Early Christian Fathers*. Vol. 1 of Library of Christian Classics. New York: Touchstone, 1996.

Suetonius. *The Twelve Caesars*. Translated by Robert Graves. New York: Penguin Classics, 1979.

Tacitus. *Annals*. In *The Historians of Ancient Rome*. Edited by Ronald Mellor. 2nd ed. New York and London: Routledge, 2004.

Tertullian. *Tertullian's Treatise on the Incarnation*. Translated by Ernest Evans. London: SPCK, 1956.

CONTEMPORARY AUTHORS

Barnes, Timothy. *Constantine and Eusebius*. Cambridge, MA: Harvard University Press, 1981.

Behr, John. *Formation of Christian Theology, Volume I: The Way to Nicea*. Crestwood, NY: St. Vladimir's Seminary Press, 2001.

Bradley, Keith. *Slavery and Society of Rome*. Cambridge: Cambridge University Press, 1994.

Bradshaw, Paul F. et al. *Essays on Hippolytus*. Bramcote, UK: Grove Books, 1978.

Brent, Allen. *Cyprian and Roman Carthage*. Cambridge: Cambridge University Press, 2010.

Brown, Raymond E. and John P. Meier. *Antioch and Rome: New Testament Cradles of Catholic Christianity*. New York: Paulist Press, 1983.

Draper, Jonathan A. "Pure Sacrifice in Didache 14 as Jewish Christian Exegesis." *Neotestamenica* 42.2 (2008): 223–52.

Evans, Craig. A. "Mark's Incipit and the Priene Calendar Inscription: From Jewish Gospel to Greco-Roman Gospel." *Journal of Greco-Roman Christianity and Judaism* 1 (2000): 67–81.

Frend, W. H. C. *The Rise of Christianity*. Philadelphia, PA: Fortress Press, 1984.

Grant, Robert M. *Greek Apologists of the Second Century*. Philadelphia, PA: The Westminster Press, 1988.

Gager, John, ed. *Curse Tablets and Binding Spells from the Ancient World*. Oxford: Oxford University Press, 1992.

Grant, Robert. *Greek Apologists of the Second Century*. Philadelphia, PA: The Westminster Press, 1988.

Hall, Stuart G. *Doctrine and Practice in the Early Church*. Grand Rapids, MI: Eerdmans, 1992.

Heffernan, Thomas J. *The Passion of Perpetua*. Oxford: Oxford University Press, 2012.

Hurtado, Larry W. *Destroyer of the Gods: Early Christian Distinctiveness in the Roman World*. Waco, TX: Baylor University Press, 2016.

Jefford, Clayton N. *Reading the Apostolic Fathers: An Introduction*. Reprint, Grand Rapids, MI: Baker Academic, 2012.

Jones, Brian W. *The Emperor Domitian*. New York: Routledge, 1993.

Kelly, J. N. D. *Early Christian Doctrines*. Rev. ed. HarperSanFrancisco, 1978.

Kraeling, Carl H. *The Christian Building: Dura Europas*. New Haven, CT: Yale University Press, 1967.

Minns, Denis. *Irenaeus: An Introduction*. London and New York: T & T Clark, 2010.

Osborn, Eric. *Irenaeus of Lyons*. Cambridge: Cambridge University Press, 2001.

Osiek, Carolyn. "Perpetua's Husband." *Journal of Early Christian Studies* 10.2 (Summer 2002): 287–90.

Otten, Willemien. "Christ's Birth of a Virgin Who Became a Wife: Flesh and Speech in Tertullian's 'De carne Christi.'" *Vigiliae Christianae* 51.3 (1997): 247–60.

Parvis, Sara and Paul Foster, eds. *Justin Martyr and His Worlds*. Minneapolis: Fortress Press, 2007.

Quasten, Johannes. *Patrology. Vol. II: The Ante-Nicene Literature After Irenaeus.* Reprint, Allen, TX: Christian Classics, 1996.

Schoedel, William R. *Ignatius of Antioch.* Philadelphia, PA: Fortress Press, 1985.

Shaw, Brent. "The Passion of Perpetua." *Past and Present* 139 (May 1993): 3–45.

Stark, Rodney. *The Rise of Christianity.* HarperSanFrancisco, 1997.

Trigg, Joseph Wilson. *Origen: The Bible and Philosophy in the Third-Century Church.* Atlanta, GA: John Knox Press, 1983.

Vall, Gregory. *Learning Christ: Ignatius of Antioch and the Mystery of Redemption.* Washington, DC: The Catholic University of America Press, 2013.

Wilken, Robert Louis. *The Christians as the Romans Saw Them.* New Haven, CT: Yale University Press, 1984.

———. *The Spirit of Early Christian Thought.* New Haven, CT: Yale University Press, 2005.

Young, Frances M. *Biblical Exegesis and the Formation of Christian Culture.* Cambridge: Cambridge University Press, 1997.